PRAISE FO

Yet again, Neil Cole has given us a gift of wisdom distilled in brilliant and wonderful simplicity. Page after page yields honey from the rock and makes the reader hungry for more and more of the ways and person of Jesus. My copy of *One Thing* is filled with underlining and highlighter markings from the introduction to the last page.

—Lance Ford
Author of *Revangelical* and *Unleader*

This is Neil Cole at his prophetic best. *One Thing* not only exposes a counterfeit religion that snares our thoughts and habits, but it refocuses our hearts and imaginations back to the liberating and revolutionary love of the One who really matters. A book to fuel movement.

—Debra Hirsch, Speaker and Author
of *Untamed* and *Redeeming Sex*

You can't go wrong if you become more and more like Jesus. And if discipleship is the process whereby we become more and more like the most holy person who ever lived, then it behooves all who claim to follow Jesus to have an ever deepening understanding of who He is and what He taught. Neil Cole does an outstanding job of reintroducing us to our wonderful Founder. This book deserves to be widely read.

—Alan Hirsch
Missional leader, author, and activist www.alanhirsch.org

At last, a book that's not just about how to change the church, but how to change the whole world! Neil Cole lifts our gaze from focusing on ecclesial debates or partisan political battles to the vision Jesus has for a world repaired, restored, and renewed under his reign. Wonderful stuff!

—Michael Frost, author *The Road to Missional*, and *Surprise the World!*

ONE THING

A Revolution to Change the World with Love

NEIL COLE

THOMAS NELSON
Since 1798

Published in Nashville, Tennessee, by Thomas Nelson. Thomas Nelson is a registered trademark of HarperCollins Christian Publishing.

Thomas Nelson titles may be purchased in bulk for educational, business, fund-raising, or sales promotional use. For information, please e-mail SpecialMarkets@ ThomasNelson.com.

Unless otherwise noted, Scripture quotations are taken from the NEW AMERICAN STANDARD BIBLE®. © 1960, 1962, 1963, 1968, 1971, 1972, 1973, 1975, 1977, 1995 by The Lockman Foundation. Used by permission.

Quotations designated NIV are from the Holy Bible, New International Version®, NIV®. Copyright ©1973, 1978, 1984, 2011 by Biblica, Inc.® Used by permission of Zondervan. All rights reserved worldwide. www.zondervan.com.

Library of Congress Control Number: 2014959033

ISBN: 978-0718-0328-6-9 (Softcover)
ISBN: 978-0718-0328-7-6 (e-book)

Printed in the United States of America

16 17 18 19 20 RRD 6 5 4 3 2 1

To those who have suffered too long under the unforgiving weight of a false, do-it-yourself gospel and are now free to be loved by Jesus and to love like Jesus. Do not let your hope for the future drown in the shame of your past. Legalists can be changed and then used to change the world. God took one and turned the world upside down. The world is now waiting for you. Be fruitful and multiply.

About Leadership ❋ Network

Leadership Network fosters innovation movements that activate the church to greater impact. We help shape the conversations and practices of pacesetter churches in North America and around the world. The Leadership Network mindset identifies church leaders with forward-thinking ideas—and helps them to catalyze those ideas resulting in movements that shape the church.

Together with HarperCollins Christian Publishing, the biggest name in Christian books, the NEXT imprint of Leadership Network moves ideas to implementation for leaders to take their ideas to form, substance, and reality. Placed in the hands of other church leaders, that reality begins spreading from one leader to the next . . . and to the next . . . and to the next, where that idea begins to flourish into a full-grown movement that creates a real, tangible impact in the world around it.

NEXT: A Leadership Network Resource
committed to helping you grow your next idea.

leadnet.org/NEXT

CONTENTS

ACKNOWLEDGMENTS

I have a friend, who has taught me much about living for my One thing. He has been my co-worker, co-author, co-founder, and pastor and has walked with me for twenty-five-plus years serving Jesus. I have received grace from him, and I have given grace because of him. His name is Phil Helfer and without his partnership in ministry I would be a much different person. Phil has read this book several times, and each time has made it a better book.

Dezi Baker has always pushed, prodded, and pulled me closer to my One thing. Dezi has fearlessly walked through the very gates of hell by my side more than once. His words are repeated several times in this work, and he deserves a shout out.

Chris Suitt and Ed Waken have given me wisdom in the formation of this book, and I am grateful for it, but more than that, they have been good friends for many years.

Mark Sweeney has represented me well these past two books, and I am appreciative. Greg Ligon and all my friends at Leadership Network have always been supportive. They have opened doors for me, and I am very grateful. I am honored to be one of the first to carry their new brand on the cover of this book. I do hope it represents them well.

I am grateful to the people at World Impact and The Oaks Conference Center who provided a quiet retreat so I could write this book.

Erin Cole, my middle-born daughter, always inspires me, encourages me, and makes me proud. Even as a tiny, towheaded toddler I could see an old soul in her green eyes looking right through me with a knowing smirk. Now as a full-grown woman, she is a deep well of insight and honesty carried in an adventurous spirit. She has given me very helpful feedback as I have written this book. May she never let go of Jesus; he is the One thing worth everything.

Dana, my bride, helped me make this book better and palatable to a much broader audience. She always keeps me honest and focused on our One thing.

Most of all there is only One who has shown me what real love is. He is my One thing. Thank you, Jesus.

Introduction

¡VIVA LA REVOLUCIÓN!

The law says, "Do this," and it is never done.
Grace says, "Believe in this," and everything is done already.
— MARTIN LUTHER

God's grace is not just an addition to our
life. It's a contradiction to our life.
— TIMOTHY KELLER

Today's world needs a revolution. Not a violent one; we've always had plenty of those. We need a revolution that changes hearts and minds with love. That is what I believe Jesus came for. It is also what I believe he has sent us here for. And it is also what I believe the world is poised to receive.

Jesus didn't come to earth just to change your Sunday morning routine. He came to change your life every day and in every way. The power of change is for every one of us, not just priests, pastors, and preachers. And everyone that is changed becomes a change agent.

Revolution is a form of the word *revolve*, and it means to turn things around. A good synonym is *repent*. Repentance (Greek, *metanoia*) means to change one's mind. It was also used as a military term. When shouted, it commanded an about-face. It can be translated as "to turn around" or "to revolve."

Christians should be revolutionaries. Our entire faith starts with a change of mind and a change of path to a new direction. We are new creations; old things have passed away and new things have come (2 Cor. 5:17).

The gospel itself is all about transformation—change. We should be the ones bringing a revolution of heart to the world. Instead, we spend our time debating theological stances, moral codes, and political issues. We quickly shout our offense at the world's values and behaviors. We are people known for resisting change. How did we get here? What will it take for us to rise up again with a real revolution of love that the story of Christ truly merits?

Let's face it: more of the same thinking will only produce more of the same activity. We need a change of mind—yesterday. We need to think and, consequently, respond differently if we hope to make any change in this world for the better. And that is what this book addresses.

The Right and the Left are growing farther apart with each passing week. Liberal politicians and conservatives are in a moral and political "take no prisoners" civil war. Each is strengthening its stance and asserting bold and often baseless accusations at the other side. This war has spilled over into all of life, not just politics, and includes the arts, education, business, journalism, science, technology, social services, military, and faith community.

Jesus said, "Blessed are the pure in heart, for they shall see God" (Matt. 5:8). Today, few are seeing God; we are not pure and undefiled in our devotion to Christ, but are full of artificial ingredients in our spirituality that make more of us and less of God. Jesus said, "Blessed are the peacemakers, for they shall be called sons of God" (Matt. 5:9). So few recognize us as children of God because we do not resemble our Father. We have not made peace but rather civil war that is anything but civil. The church is posturing itself farther and farther away from any positive influence in society, because it is deeply rooted in a moralistic crusade and quite comfortable shouting at the world from a distance. We should be on a transformative, redemptive mission of peace and love like Jesus the revolutionary, but instead we take stands, pass laws, and campaign against issues. Instead of changing the world with the power of love, we react to issues and take defensive postures and look as hateful as any faction in this growing divide. The civil war is hot, and neither side is at all close to building bridges or bringing peace. We simply must take a different approach if we want to make a difference in this world—and now is the time! But in order to make a difference, we must first be different ourselves.

Today's emerging generation is fed up with an unengaged, judgmental Christianity that is afraid to get its hands dirty with real change but is more than willing to tell everyone else how bad they are.

In his book *Revangelical*, Lance Ford asks us an important question:

> What evangelical is supposed to mean—bringer of good news— is completely different from what it has come to mean for many in our society: judgmental, misogynist, bigoted, homophobic. How did this happen? How did the "good news" people come to be widely regarded as bad news?[1]

As the church conversation has shifted from church growth to becoming missional to the world, it is imperative that the core issues of the gospel—transformation and acting out of love—infuse the discussion. This book addresses that need. Our message is good news; our presence should be good news. Because we are not good news to society, I propose that we have lost our identity and sacrificed our core message.

We have had unrealistic expectations of imposing morality without spirituality in a world that desires spirituality without morality. We are surprised that the unredeemed act like they are unredeemed, but the real shock is how the redeemed act like they are *not*. This book is a call to the church to respond in love toward the world and not to impose our own values on others but rather live them out. Grounded in the love found in the new covenant, this book will passionately call the church back to its true spiritual roots and provide tangible examples of how that was done in the past, by our founder himself, and can be done today.

Christians are tired of being the laughingstock of late-night television. They are also angered by the poor results the church is seeing as it seeks to be a transformative presence in society. This book will appeal to Christians who are tired of being characterized by the world as angry people known only for what they are against. It offers an alternative that is biblical, effective, subversive, and loving, all at the same time.

We are so busy with so many things. To a busy lady, Jesus once said, "Martha, Martha, you are worried and bothered about so many things; but only one thing is necessary" (Luke 10:41-42). Paul echoed that same idea in Philippians when he said, "But one thing I do: forgetting what lies behind and reaching forward to what lies ahead, I press on toward the goal for the prize of the upward call of God in Christ Jesus" (Phil. 3:13–14). He also instructed the Galatians, who were carrying the heavy burden of all the laws of the Old Testament: "For the whole Law is fulfilled in one word, in the statement, 'You shall love your neighbor as yourself'" (Gal. 5:14).

It is time for us to trade in our busy religion with so many rules and causes we are staunchly against for a "one thing" spirituality. That one thing is the love that is generated by being with Jesus, being focused upon Jesus, and letting Jesus leak out in our lives.

If the apostle Paul could send a letter to the Western church today, what would he say? I think he would re-send the book of Galatians to a large segment of our community. I will attempt to demonstrate why I feel that way as this book unfolds. What is very important is that we realize that being like the Galatian church is not okay. Neither Paul nor Jesus felt that being good in your own strength is something to give an approving nod to. Galatians is a harsh word for a sad situation. It addresses the very basis of our entire spiritual well-being and is nothing less than a playbook for a spiritual revolution.

In his commentary on the apostle's letter, Richard Longenecker wrote the following:

> Paul's Galatians is, in fact, like a lion turned loose in the arena of Christianity. It challenges, intimidates, encourages, and focuses our attention on what is really essential as little else can. How we deal with the issues it raises and the teachings it presents will in large measure determine how we think as Christians and how we live as Christ's own.[2]

It is my intent in this book to let that lion out once again to do its work on the counterfeit Christianity we have become

familiar and perhaps even a little too comfortable with. Galatians
is, indeed, a revolutionary manifesto.

There are two sections to this book that build from the internal revolution within our own soul to then bringing that change
to the world around us. The first section is drawn from Galatians
and the second from the Gospels; we will learn from both Paul and
Jesus. The first section will tell us what it means to be Christ like;
the latter section will show what Christ was like as he addressed
some very important issues we face today.

Writing a book that focuses its first half on Paul's Galatians
and second half on Christ in the Gospels may seem at first to be
forced together. However, I actually believe these two parts do,
and must, join together as one thing. It is not enough to have a
change of heart and not bring that change to a dying world. It is
also not sufficient to try to change the world and leave your own
life unchanged in the process.

The first half of this book exposes our hearts and failed
spirituality. The latter half gives us the only real flesh and blood
alternative to our current mess.

Incarnation is a popular term today in a church that talks
about being missional. This book is all about the incarnation of
Christ lived out in the world. First we must stop putting forth a
fake and lifeless spirituality and surrender our whole being to the
true one-thing spirituality that is found within us. Then we must
emulate the life of Christ and respond to our world the way he did.
It is time to let Christ out of the box and let him loose in the world
by our faith working though love.

There is a wave of scholarship attempting to separate Paul
from Jesus. I am a firm believer that neither Paul nor Jesus would
be in favor of such a division. Paul's one focus was on Jesus (1 Cor.

2:2). Jesus is Paul's "one thing" (Phil. 3:13–14). Paul puts Jesus first, and that is what made Paul who he was. This book is written with the assumption that Paul and Jesus are of one mind and one heart. The intent of the book is that we also have that same heart and mind as we approach the world we live in. If we have the one-thing spirituality that Paul described in Galatians, I believe we will live more like Christ in this world. The spiritual life Paul addressed and the life Christ lived as an example in the Gospels is indeed one thing. This book is structured to demonstrate this thinking.

The very nature of a revolution requires that one address the reason for abandoning the status quo in favor of a better future. For that reason, much of the first section of the book will deconstruct a faith that lacks potency and produces a less-than-loving Christianity. But a revolution that only deconstructs is damaging, short-lived, and certainly not remembered favorably. So the rest of the book will cast the vision for what can be and, in my opinion, should be.

A turnaround requires that we not only turn away from something but also turn toward something else. The Bible often speaks of this action. It uses language such as "repent and believe" or "put off the old and put on the new." There is a valid and important place for deconstructing the old before we reconstruct the new. This book will do both.

This book is not ammunition for any side of a cultural war of values and political ideals. It is, instead, hope for all sides. It will challenge us to stop fighting political battles and take up a spiritual one. True change happens in our hearts and minds, not the halls of legislation or the electronic platform of media. There is indeed only one thing that can bring true change to this world, and that is Jesus.

Section 1

THE REVOLUTION
OF A HEART

Chapter 1

A TALE OF TWO CHURCHES

If you can't show the difference between religion and the
gospel, people will confuse morality with a changed heart.
—Timothy Keller

It is Christ alone that we need. A Christ
supplemented is a Christ supplanted.
—J. Vernon McGee

There once were two churches that couldn't be more different. One church strove hard to do everything right. The other
was always confused about which way was right, so, instead, it let
everyone do something wrong. We will call the church that did
good "the good church" and the other "the bad church."

At the good church, everyone was in agreement and submitted
to "spiritual" leadership. At the bad church, everyone had a different opinion over who was the right leader. Consequently it was
hard to find any direction at all. They were divided.

Those in the good church were very committed to the
Scriptures and did all they could to obey them. In the bad church

there was open immorality, which included adultery and even incestuous relationships.

Religious rituals were very important in the good church, and they were well known for their sacrifice and commitment to keeping God's sacraments. In the bad church, the Lord's Supper became a wild party where people got drunk on the communion wine and hoarded all the food.

To see how sharply the apostle Paul addressed legalism, one must only compare two of his church plants that could not be further apart: the Galatians (the good church) and the Corinthians (the bad church).

One of these churches was notorious for its sin. The other was renown for its righteousness. The Corinthian church was infected by immorality of such a kind that even the pagans cringed. A man was sleeping with his father's wife, and not in secret. The Corinthians, instead, reveled in their tolerance (1 Cor. 5:1–2). This church had much confusion over sexuality, and as a result, there was a lot of sleeping around among church members (1 Cor. 5:9–11). There were divisions in the church over celebrity leaders. The people fought over whom each aligned with and whose name (or brand) they would bear (1 Cor. 1:10–17). There were class distinctions in the Corinthian church. The people turned the Lord's Supper and the church gathering into a wild party where people actually got drunk and encouraged strange phenomena to occur. They left the poor without anything to conduct the Lord's Supper while the wealthy became drunk on the wine served to remember Jesus' sacrifice (1 Cor. 11:17–22). These people questioned Paul's apostolic gift and started to follow some leaders who wanted to be large and in charge. This church was out of control and full of sin. Paul had to write at least three letters to them to correct them (1

Cor. 5:9).[1] There is no doubt Corinth was a messed-up church and needed a lot of help.

The Galatian church, on the other hand, did everything right. They wouldn't tolerate evil and strove only to do what was good. They were strict people of the book and were willing to pay huge personal costs to be obedient to the things of God. All who knew them would immediately recognize them as highly committed to their beliefs and willing to sacrifice for them.

We could easily be tempted to think of these churches as the good church and the bad church. If we were writing corrective epistles to these churches today, we would likely be tempted to commend the one's striving to do right and only mention some of their faults in a most generous and forgiving manner. We would also be tempted to address the Corinthians with harsh words and try to shame them into conforming to godliness.

What is remarkable is that Paul does the opposite. While he definitely corrects both churches, only one of these churches was so off that the corrective letter does not contain a single nice word. To the Galatians (the good church), he doesn't have a positive remark. He called them foolish, bewitched, and deserters of Christ. He didn't commend anything they were doing, but actually called all their efforts cursed. To the Galatians, Paul barely gave a pleasant greeting (Gal. 1:1–5), which nonetheless is dripping with instruction. He seemed to jump right into the problem and not mince his words or soften his language.

One of Paul's favorite terms for people in the church was *hagioi* ("saints"), which literally means "holy ones." This term appears multiple times in almost all his letters to the churches. To the Corinthians, with blatant immorality in their midst, he referred to them as "holy ones" eleven times. There is only one letter to the churches where Paul does not use the term even once: Galatians. Those who strove most to be holy were not worthy to be called saints. Those who were filled with divisions, immorality, and doctrinal confusion, he called saints more often than any other church.

Paul wrote corrective epistles to both churches, the Galatians and the Corinthians, so neither is as it should be, but we find his letter to the "good church" to be far more abrupt and harsh than the letters written to the Corinthians. We would be tempted to think the Galatians only needed a few tweaks to be fine, and the Corinthians needed an entire overhaul from top to bottom. But actually it is the Galatians who receive the overhaul of all things, and the Corinthians get a series of tweaks and adjustments.

THE GALATIANS

Galatians was not written to a single church but to the churches of a region. I lean toward the southern Galatian theory, which identifies the recipients as the churches Paul and Barnabas started on their first missionary journey in southeastern Asia Minor. I believe this was one of Paul's first letters, written perhaps right after that first missionary journey and before the Jerusalem council of Acts 15.[2]

These churches were left leaderless by Paul and Barnabas and easily succumbed to the influence of some legalistic Jewish Christians that theologians call Judaizers. It was in this region that Paul was stoned, where he met and started mentoring Timothy, and where Barnabas and Paul first saw the incredible response among the Gentiles to the gospel.[3]

The Galatians received Paul's gospel by faith and with great enthusiasm. They were saved by grace through faith, just as most evangelical churches today claim. Their heresy was not about their original salvation experience, as we would struggle with Jehovah's Witnesses or perhaps even some Roman Catholics who would require works that earn salvation. Their problem came after salvation, as they began to think that growing in spirituality was a by-product of doing good works on their own initiative. They were instructed by the Judaizers to become Jews after their conversion by keeping all that was instructed in the Old Testament. This being one of the first mission outposts in the Gentile world, it was important that they stay with the gospel and not be bewitched into becoming Jewish proselytes. Paul fought hard for the gospel and was willing to stand up to all, even the apostle Peter (Gal. 2:11–21). He would not rest for "even an hour" (Gal. 2:5) in defending the good news that he was given by Jesus himself (Gal. 1:11–13).

THE GREATEST HERESY

In the halls of theological education, most discussions regarding the heresies that were threats to the New Testament–era churches tend to land squarely on the lies of Gnosticism. Many scholars see the New Testament writings primarily addressing Gnosticism. I agree that Gnosticism was a problem worth addressing, and in many ways it is a heresy that is still causing damage, but I strongly disagree that it was the primary heretical threat of New Testament times. Without question, the heresy most strongly written against in the New Testament is what we typically call legalism.

Why do our theologians so quickly jump to Gnosticism as the major threat of the New Testament? For one thing, I believe the two heresies can be joined together and feed off of one another. But I also believe legalism is overlooked because we ourselves are so invested in that form of spirituality that we cannot see it for what it really is. A fish in water can hardly understand that it is wet and cannot see any other fish as wet either. But they are wet. Our viewpoint is skewed by our environment, which is so full of legalistic views of spirituality that we do not recognize what is all around us. My hope in writing this book is to expose that. We must have a revolution.

In fact, as I mention the word *legalism*, most readers will quickly think about cults and false religions that are opposed to our gospel of salvation by grace through faith. Legalism seems confined to simply a works-based salvation as opposed to salvation by grace through faith. We think we settled our view on this, listed it in our creeds, and now we can go about our spiritual lives without giving it another thought. We barely pay attention to Galatians, because we have already been saved by grace through faith. We have canonized and defended the doctrine and are no longer vulnerable to the problems of the Galatians. This view gives us a false sense of security and blinds us to some very serious lies that are pandemic in our churches.

The Galatian churches were saved by grace through faith and would say as much if they had a statement of faith, but they were also legalistic. Paul even said to them, "Are you so foolish? Having begun by the Spirit [saved by grace through faith], are you now being perfected by the flesh [human-generated spirituality]?" (Gal. 3:3).

ONE THING

| 8 |

GALATIANISM: A DO-IT-YOURSELF SPIRITUALITY

We fail to see that much of our actions are indeed tainted by the same error of the Galatian heresy. The Galatians seemed to accept that salvation is secured by faith in the gospel, but a spiritual walk thereafter is based on our own efforts to live godly lives. That is as much a legalistic theology as any cult that says we must merit our salvation and work hard for it. Perhaps it is best that we call it something else, because we have put legalism in such a small container and allowed so much of Galatianism to run loose in our churches. I suggest a better term is *do-it-yourself spirituality*.

In the book of Galatians, Paul used the example of Abram's quest to have the son of promise to demonstrate two competing ways of fulfilling our spiritual purposes—the flesh versus the Spirit (Gal. 4:21–31). This example is a great way to demonstrate that the issue at the heart of Galatians is not just works salvation but is, in fact, attempting to fulfill God's promise with our own ingenuity and effort.

As the story goes, decades after receiving the promise of a son, Abram's wife, Sarai, remained barren. Eventually they decided to help God with the promise and chose for Abram to have a child with Sarai's servant, Hagar. Abram and Hagar did indeed have a son, but it was not the fulfillment of God's promise. Rather, it was the product of a human attempting to do what only God can, without the miraculous.

This example goes to the heart of the issue that the Galatians letter addresses. Frankly, Abram didn't break the law by having a son with Hagar. Paul actually points out that Abram lived 430 years before the law was written (Gal. 3:17). What Abram did in the story was to stop believing in God's ability or desire to fulfill his promise. Instead, Abram took matters into his own hands. He lacked faith, and the result was that he did things his own way and with his own strength. He set out to fulfill God's will with his own ingenuity and plans, void of God's miracle.

This is a prime example of human-generated spirituality— when we set out to accomplish God's plans in our own abilities. This is the Galatian heresy at its core.

In the Galatians' day, their do-it-yourself spirituality was indeed returning to keeping the law in all its details. But there are more ways to act out in human-generated spirituality than just keeping the law, just as Abram did (430 years before the law).

In order to receive the full impact of Galatians, we need to understand that do-it-yourself spirituality can take many different forms. We may not argue over circumcision, but we are just as guilty of relying on our own abilities and plans rather than having faith in God's miraculous promise to accomplish what he said he would. Human-generated spirituality is pandemic in our churches today, even though we are not arguing over the law and have settled that salvation is by grace through faith.

The way we do ministry is plagued by human engineering. Programs are intended to make people more spiritual. We publish curriculums that are designed to make people more faithful. Models of church are intended to entice attenders. We have systems upon systems to accomplish what only God can do. In fact, most of what we call discipleship in our churches is merely an attempt to form people's knowledge base and conform their behaviors to align with what we think is spiritual. The results are really just theological moralists lacking true spiritual power.

The results, beyond church attendance and proud pew sitters, are pitiful, to say the least. We put faith in strategies of evangelism that are thought to be more effective than others. Pragmatism rather than the power of the gospel drives the evangelistic process in many churches. If we do the process right, we believe, we are guaranteed a higher rate of conversions per gospel presentation. All of these types of ministry exercises reek of human engineering and quickly lose sight of the miracle of God's promise and power.

A FALSE-GOSPEL SPIRITUALITY

We can apply this false spirituality and gain many accolades and lose relatively few things. We are so driven by pragmatism—after all, we're really trying to do good things—that we are easily seduced toward a false-gospel spirituality.

In fact, this form of spirituality is quite compatible with almost everything we do. Really, the only thing that is sacrificed by a false gospel is the true gospel. With that sacrifice, we lose everything that is important and keep a lot of things we think are important but have no real value. We do not lose our churches, our leadership, our finances, our buildings, our branding, our statements of faith, our creeds, our organization, our numerical success; even most of our theology is kept in tact with this false-gospel spirituality. All we really lose is everything most important, namely, Jesus (Gal. 5:2–4). Authentic spiritual life is also lost (Gal. 5:6; 6:15). With that, any real impact on the world is lost and replaced with organizations doing supposedly good things. What we lose is what is most important: faith working through love.

Paul said:

For in Christ Jesus neither circumcision nor uncircumcision has any value. The only thing that counts is faith expressing itself through love. (Gal. 5:6 NIV)

If we can do church without a faith that expresses itself through love, what do we actually have in the end? I'm convinced we are really quite content with a spirituality that lacks faith expressed through love. We would rather have a statement of faith than real faith that works its way into our lives as love. So we have redefined faith as merely accenting a list of doctrinal statements that we can agree with. We call that "belief," but it has nothing to do with actually living by a faith that works its way into our words and deeds as love.

For my part, I do not want anything to do with a Christianity void of love. But most people in the world already know the dirty little secret: our churches are not driven by faith working itself out in love. We can say otherwise, but nobody hears us, because our lack of love shouts so loudly in our posture, priorities, and practices. In much of Christendom we have replaced an authentic spirituality with behavior conformed to a moral standard and accepted that as a Christian life.

Recently I was asked to do some teaching and coaching for the Salvation Army. I noticed that wine was left off the table at our meals, which is not uncommon in *churchianity*. Like many Christian organizations, officers in the Salvation Army sign a covenant to abstain from alcoholic beverages for as long as they are commissioned in that organization. Not to single out the Salvation Army, this is a scenario played out in many Christian groups, from

Southern Baptists to Nazarenes and many parachurch organizations and Christian colleges.

When you think about this, Jesus himself would not qualify for leadership (even membership) in many denominations. That is neither a surprise nor shocking, but it is extremely questionable. When we have come so far that the founder and finisher of our faith (Heb. 12:1–3) would not be welcome as a member of the organization that bears his name, then you know we have wandered too far down a twisted rabbit hole. That is, however, where we find ourselves, and this book is written in an attempt to right that trajectory.

At this dinner with my Salvation Army friends, we began to discuss the issue of abstaining from alcohol. To their credit, the argument for abstinence was not that drinking alcohol was a sin or that abstaining makes one more righteous. According to our conversation, today's "Salvos" abstain from alcohol to be seen as different from the world rather than conforming to it. Since they have a strong ministry to addicts on the street, they do not want to put a stumbling block in the way of broken people who are trying to find healing from addictive lives.

Admirable as that is, a few questions still arise: Was Jesus seen as different from his world? Of course he was. Is abstaining from alcohol the unique difference we really want to put forward to this world? Was Jesus someone who caused others to stumble when he partook of wine or even supplied it in abundance for a wedding reception (John 2:1–11)?

Another reason for this mandatory commitment to abstain from alcohol is that the covenant had been put in place by one of the founders of the movement. Let's be honest; to change it would violate way too many sacred cows. It is now a cultural mainstay that appears immutable. But that is a subject for another book. I love my coworkers in the Salvation Army and Southern Baptists and Nazarenes and have loads of respect for their ministries. My point is that we try to manage people's spirituality externally. This management tends to produce a context in which Jesus would not be welcomed. We are often guilty of excluding the founder of our faith to maintain the sacred cow established by the founder of our denomination.

I recently spoke at a Christian organization and submitted a receipt for a meal I had while there. The receipt I turned in didn't have the itemization of what was ordered, so the office at first was reticent to reimburse it, because I potentially could have had alcohol. I assured them that out of respect for their wishes I did not. But rules are rules, so they declined. I told them I would buy my own meal, but I also mentioned that lying about having alcohol so that I would get money was actually far worse than if I actually had a glass of wine. They reimbursed the meal.

Do not hear me wrong. It is not a bad thing to abstain from alcohol, and, in fact, it can be a good thing for many people. Alcoholism can be devastating and can destroy many lives. I should know.

I actually should be someone who reacts against alcohol abuse and advocates abstinence. I come from a long line of addicts on both sides of my family. My paternal grandfather and grandmother struggled with alcoholism. My maternal grandmother was a prescription drug addict. My mother was a chain smoker and died of cancer at an early age. My father was an alcoholic while I was growing up. To his credit, he sobered up while I was in college, but by then I was out of the home for good, with all my emotional scars intact.

My family is not the only reason I should be an advocate of abstinence. One of the first church planters in our movement was a very creative and entrepreneurial leader and artist. The church he helped plant was even featured in the seminal book *The Shaping of Things to Come* by Alan Hirsch and Mike Frost.[4] It was an innovative missional church in an artistic community spinning off small businesses with creative ideas, inventions, and ministries to unusual people. The church planter began to struggle with alcoholism and prescription drugs. Like all such addictions, he went though bouts of intoxication and seasons of sobriety. During one binge, we arranged to take him to a rehabilitation facility. The very morning we were to pick him up, he was found dead of an overdose. He left behind a young family with small children. Who knows what impact he might have had if addictions hadn't consumed his life?

One of my apprentices whom I led to Christ and who subsequently led many to Christ himself now lives on the street, addicted to meth. He lost his wife, his home, his business, his friends, his church, his health, his sleep, his sanity, and his teeth because he became a slave of chemicals instead of Christ. And there are more stories like that I can tell of people who once were vibrant agents of God's kingdom all over the world but who lost everything because of alcohol or drugs.

I personally know the cost of addiction. I fully sympathize with the covenant of the Salvation Army. Nevertheless I have chosen not to react against alcohol by advocating a life of abstinence. While I've not personally been intoxicated by drugs or alcohol, I do not abstain from alcohol or enforce such rules on others. Why? That is the important question that has motivated the writing of this book, but it goes far deeper than simply teetotaling. If one believes that abstaining from alcohol is a means to a deeper spiritual life, then legalism is at the core of his or her belief, and likely, it is unseen. I'm not saying that those who choose abstinence are legalists, for in many cases that is a wise discipline. I'm saying that those who establish and enforce policies for others to abstain are using the law to accomplish what only the gospel can do. Those who feel such steps are a path to spirituality are under the delusion of legalism. That is the Galatian problem Paul addresses so firmly and uses a variety of terms to communicate.

The false gospel of human-generated spirituality was addressed by both Jesus and Paul with the strongest of words. Entire books of the Bible are directed solely at the dismantling of this theological persuasion, including Romans, Galatians, and Hebrews. You cannot find more harsh words from Jesus or Paul than those directed against a legalistic mind-set. Jesus called legalists "hypocrites," "white washed tombs," and "the blind leading the blind." Paul's words are just as charged and perhaps even more graphic.

The language Paul used to describe someone under the burden of a do-it-yourself spirituality is related specifically to the Galatian context, but do not think it doesn't apply to us today. He uses the term *circumcision* as a symbol of one living under legalistic rule. A young man in Galatia at the time may have wished that circumcision was only symbolic; nevertheless in Galatians, Paul used this one act as symbolic of living an entire life under the lordship of rules and rituals rather than by the Spirit of God. When he spoke of circumcision, he did not intend to only address one specific command of the Old Testament (or only men); it is characteristic of the entire law. While we are far removed from debating the merits of being circumcised today, understand that Paul means more than simply the act itself. The term has a comprehensive reach that includes all of our physical efforts to live spiritual lives.

Paul also referred to *the flesh* as an expression meaning someone living according to human effort rather than by the Spirit. More often than not, when we hear "the flesh," we go quickly in our thoughts to sensual and even sexual temptations, which is far too narrow for Paul's usage. When the apostle used "the flesh" to describe something, he was saying that the strength for the effort is found within our own bodies rather than by the Spirit of Christ.

A third way that Paul refers to human-generated spirituality is the usage of the term *the law*. As we shall see later in another chapter, Paul classifies all activity into two categories: the law and the Spirit, and the two cannot in any way be mixed to fruitful affect. It is important for us to understand that the law, as Paul used it, is applied to more than simply the Old Testament, but to all the rules and traditions established by the religious leaders of the day. This opens up our application of Galatians to a more meaningful and specific set of problems in our churches today. We, too, give holy merit to traditions passed down from our elders, even though they are not in Scripture. We also attempt to make people holier by laying down rules and standards to follow. To a great extent, this is what Paul meant when he speaks of the law.

It is important that we delineate these words because we have a tendency to take terms literally and specifically and miss the broader applications. I know personally that for a long time I did not really appreciate Galatians as I should have simply because I didn't see myself as struggling with trying to obey Old Testament law or arguing over the merits of circumcision. When we limit the message of Galatians to such stringent applications, we miss the message of this profound book for today.

THE TRUE GOSPEL CHANGES EVERYTHING

Many in recent days have written against the idea that the gospel and resulting salvation is merely a ticket to heaven after death. Indeed, the gospel is the beginning of life in the here and now and not just the hereafter. I like to think that I also have been a prophet calling for such a change. But I fear this view is only part of the solution. Our shallow view of the gospel and salvation sees it as a reservation in the afterlife rather than a life without reservation in God's kingdom now. The consequence of this cheap gospel is that it is something to secure right away and then go about your life as normal, until the gift is redeemed after you die. Herein is the other half of the problem: we live out our spiritual lives in our own capacities rather than letting this true gospel work out from within us.

Eternal life, by its basic definition, cannot be something that just happens after death. If indeed it is eternal, it is as much now as it will be then. The gospel and our life are something we must be living right now.

As I was starting churches among some of life's most broken and marginalized people, I often found that the lure of sin would recapture some of the new members. It was always sad to watch people who were once free return to the gutter. Many leaders in the new churches suggested I increase the levels of external pressure to keep people on the narrow path. I fully understood that desire, but I refused. My answer was always the same: *I believe that grace is better at changing lives than the rule of law.* I would much rather err on the side of grace than venture into the mire of legalism and man-made spirituality. I would not chase people down who have chosen to walk away from Jesus and try to make them want to be spiritual. That has never been my role. I could not play the role of the Holy Spirit for others. God respects people's choices. Who am I to not respect them as well? If the love and life of Jesus is not enough for people, I'm pretty sure my rules, guilt, and shame are not going to be enough.

Using legalistic methods to modify behavior is a resort to a false spirituality based on a false gospel, and it does not result in true fruit. If the true gospel of grace is insufficient, then all other efforts will be meaningless in the end. All that is not done in love is meaningless (1 Cor. 13:1–13).

Perhaps that explains the difference in the ways Paul addressed these two very different churches. The Corinthians, in all their messed-up chaos, understood grace and valued it far more than the Galatians, who possessed a self-righteous delusion. It wasn't that the sins of the Corinthians were less than those of the Galatians; it was that the Corinthians were more likely to recognize they were wrong and accept God's grace to change. Perhaps this explains the harsh tone Paul used with the self-righteous Galatians, because they needed to be shocked into an awareness of their wrong choices. It wasn't the type or amount of sin that was the issue as much as it was the openness to acknowledge sin.

In much the same way, Jesus also seemed to give far more grace to the sinful and broken and was harsh by comparison to the self-righteous spiritual leaders of his day. He even said to them, "Truly I say to you that the tax collectors and prostitutes will get into the kingdom of God before you" (Matt. 21:31). How scandalous was that?

Mark described one encounter in this way:

When the scribes of the Pharisees saw that He was eating with the sinners and tax collectors, they said to His disciples, "Why is He eating and drinking with tax collectors and sinners?" And hearing this, Jesus said to them, "It is not those who are healthy who need a physician, but those who are sick; I did not come to call the righteous, but sinners." (Mark 2:16–17)

Is it possible that being moral can be just as bad as being immoral from a spiritual perspective? Wow, let that question simmer for a moment. Can it be that the "moral majority" at the tea party on the Right is no better than the Left who tolerate all forms of immorality . . . except of course being conservative morally?

Both the Corinthians and the Galatians had sin issues that needed to be addressed. The sins of one were not worse than the sins of the other. While that may sound right to us, it wouldn't sound right to the Galatians, would it? Those who are working so hard to do the right thing at great personal sacrifice (e.g. adult circumcision) would never accept that they are as guilty as those who are obviously and openly engaging in sexual immorality.

In our Christian culture today, sexual sin is at the top of the list of capital offenses. That, however, is not the way the New Testament views spirituality. Acting morally superior to those who are sexually immoral is, in fact, treated more harshly. Why? Because it is deluded, harmful to many more people, far removed from love, is a counterfeit to the true gospel, and is difficult to recognize as sin. We need to treat self-righteousness with more harshness than sexual immorality if we want to resemble a New Testament spiritual climate.

I have found that self-righteousness is as forgivable as any other sin; it just isn't as recognizable as other sins. To many it looks "good" and, therefore, is acceptable. Why should a "good church" need to make huge changes? Those deceived by a do-it-yourself spirituality are not just unaware of their sin, but they are actually seduced into valuing the sin. Therein lies the deadly poison. It takes a harsh slap in the face to awaken such a person.

Jesus and Paul shook up those who were under this delusion with a brash jolt of love. A harsh slap seems the only way to get them to wake up. We tend to think that harsh words are not loving or godly and prefer to use nice words and a gentle nudge . . . usually to no avail. Is it really loving to let people continue to digest poison because we do not want to risk people thinking we are mean? I think that is not loving but selfish. There are times when a harsh word is the most Christlike thing we can do because the consequences of self-righteousness are so damaging to so many people.

There are deep, deadly, and far-reaching symptoms that are born from digesting the poison of self-righteousness in the body of Christ. In the next chapter I will draw ten consequences from Galatians for buying into a do-it-yourself spirituality. It will become clear that we also face these same consequences in abundance in our church world today. We can and should learn more from this ancient letter to an allegedly good church.

Chapter 2

CONSEQUENCES OF A DO-IT-YOURSELF SPIRITUALITY

*God is looking for people through whom He can
do the impossible. What a pity that we plan only
the things that we can do by ourselves.*
—A. W. TOZER

*If your god never disagrees with you, you might be
worshipping an idealized version of yourself.*
—TIMOTHY KELLER

My neighborhood seems to be under invasion. My home is
being surrounded by warehouse stores full of do-it-yourself
(DIY) tools and products. Within six miles of my house are seven
such stores! In fact, they all seem to be doing good business even
though they are all pretty much the same. Evidence of DIY stores
can be seen in every room of my house as well. There are not
just television shows dedicated to the DIY revolution but entire
networks dedicated to it twenty-four hours a day. But the DIY
revolution is not just happening in our culture; it has even invaded

our view of spirituality, and there are dire consequences of a DIY spirituality.

To bring to light the reasons why a do-it-yourself approach to spirituality is so wrong, I will list ten consequences from Paul's letter to the Galatians demonstrating that a human-generated approach to spirituality doesn't work and has negative consequences for all. Any single consequence below should be enough to warn us. But these ten consequences, as you will see, are not independent of one another but actually build upon one another with momentum. In other words, the DIY spirituality cannot be simply contained in a single category, but like a weed it spreads until it takes over everything. All of these consequences were evident in the Galatian churches, and they are also rampant today in our own churches in a different but similar way.

1. PRIDE AND SELF-DECEPTION START US DOWN THE WRONG PATH

> *For if anyone thinks he is something when he is nothing, he deceives himself. . . . Do not be deceived, God is not mocked; for whatever a man sows, this he will also reap.* (Gal. 6:3, 7)

Paul says to the churches of Galatia, "You foolish Galatians, who has bewitched you?" (3:1). Once you start down the path of do-it-yourself spirituality you have already crossed over into a self-deceived state of being. The deception is specifically rooted in a pride that makes you think you are immune to consequences. Somehow you feel you are special and can get away with things that others will not (6:7). How else can you explain the type of hypocrisy that is so prevalent? It is like a spell cast over us. We become "bewitched."

When we are doing something good, we feel good about it. Unfortunately that hurts us in many ways. It makes us resistant to correction, and we become defensive about what we are doing. We take correction personally and quickly become offended at any suggestion that we are wrong. Those who point out that we may be guilty of functioning in the flesh are seen as unloving, unsupportive, and perhaps even divisive. Paul wrote, "So have I become your enemy by telling you the truth?" (4:16). Often truth tellers become enemies of those who are under the spell of DIY spirituality.

The sinister problem with self-deception is that you are completely unaware when it is happening. If you knew you were deceived, you would do something about it, but because you are blind to the problem, the issue continues to do damage. Doing good can be the enemy of being good.

This deluded sense of being better than others is a predominant problem with do-it-yourself Christians. For instance, it is common to meet people who suffer from what I call the Martha syndrome. Like the harried woman in the gospel story (Luke 10:38–42), this person is hardworking, doing good things for everyone else, and trying to hold it all together. She is busy and hospitable, so she likely feels she is in the right. Mary, on the other hand, is not doing anything but listening to Jesus, so Martha asks Jesus to tell Mary to help her out. This is a reasonable request for a busy sister who needs some assistance. Jesus doesn't comply but actually rebukes Martha for being consumed with so many unimportant things and missing out on the most important thing: Jesus being in her home.

There are many Marthas in the church today, and frankly they are usually leading things and being admired for it. In most churches,

Martha would get a plaque because she is working hard, doing good, and making everyone else feel good. In those same churches, Mary would be rebuked. This hectic busyness results in fatigue and stress, which is a problem according to Jesus, but a praiseworthy practice according to most churches. Jesus, however, was not impressed.

The Martha syndrome is the fact that most who suffer from the same stressful extreme of Martha actually prefer it over the relaxing and spiritually enriching practices of Mary. When the story is presented to someone who suffers from the Martha syndrome, he or she still prefers Martha's way over Mary's—and Jesus'. People justify this by passionately proclaiming, "If we don't act like Martha, nothing will ever get done in the church!"

The Martha syndrome is a self-delusion born from thinking more highly of yourself than you ought to. In fact, I'm confident there are some reading these words right now who are probably justifying Martha in their own minds. I know it, because the Martha syndrome is strongly pervasive in the Western church. It is a deception that is hard to break because it means you have to admit that all the good you are doing is not good at all. All that you think is so important is meaningless compared to the one thing that is really important. That is hard for someone who has spent so long doing good to accept. This is a deluded sense that you think you are better than you really are and you would prefer not to change. That is a serious problem.

For some, you may want to take a moment to read the story in Luke's gospel and honestly ask yourself if you had a choice of being a Mary, who rests at the feet of Jesus, listening to his every word, or a Martha, who keeps everything organized and running, which would you choose? If you honestly prefer to be Martha and feel Jesus and Mary just don't get it, you are suffering from the Martha syndrome—you are spiritually deluded. This story in Luke can actually be a litmus test of delusion when talking about DIY spirituality. What you choose to do with that revelation is up to you.

When you are deceived, something you think is true is, in fact, not true at all, but you don't know it. Some problems you know about and can address if you have the courage to do so. Self-deception is sinister because you do not know about it. If you knew about it, you would fix it.

Being deceived is like walking around all day with your fly open. Often what is obvious to everyone else is lost to you. Unless someone tells you, the problem will continue to be exposed to all but the one with the problem.

A delusional problem that goes on unaddressed will likely get worse as time passes. Such is self-deception. It is the gateway to every other evil consequence of do-it-yourself spirituality that follows. Just as deception led Eve to eat the fruit and give it to her husband, deception is the gateway influence that opens us up to all sorts of evil . . . without our ever really knowing how bad we are until it is too late. A deluded mind cannot think its way out of the box it is in. The deluded mind *is* the problem, so it cannot fix the problem. We must be exposed and shocked out of this delusional state. That explains why Paul used such harsh language when addressing the Galatians. The first responses to correction for a self-deceived mind are defensiveness and then accusations. The one who sees the glaring problem and needs to correct it has to break through this initial defensiveness, and that requires some level of jarring.

I once spoke to a group of pastors about this subject using some of the letters Jesus wrote to the seven churches of Asia Minor (three of which were deluded) and felt I needed to boldly grab their attention. So I stood before them and started teaching—with my fly open (there were no women in the audience). I had arranged for a friend in the crowd to let me know right away that my zipper was down. I didn't realize how much power I had given him until I saw him just sitting there, smiling at me as I kept speaking and standing there exposed and vulnerable. Eventually he spoke up and said that my fly was open.

I exaggeratedly turned around to correct the problem, and on my back was a taped sign: Kick Me. To add even more drama to the scenario, I also had a long piece of toilet paper hanging from my pants. I used my humiliation to shock my listeners into recognizing that self-deception is nasty and makes fools of us. I wanted them to see how ugly self-deception can be. The first consequence of a do-it-yourself spirituality is the deluded idea that you can do it yourself. You think more highly of yourself than you ought to think. The next consequence is that because you can do it, you have to do it all . . . or all is lost.

2. PERFECTION DRIVES US . . . OR ALL IS LOST

For as many as are of the works of the Law are under a curse;
for it is written, "Cursed is everyone who does not abide by all
things written in the book of the Law, to perform them." . . .

Behold I, Paul, say to you that if you receive circumcision,
Christ will be of no benefit to you. And I testify again to
every man who receives circumcision, that he is under
obligation to keep the whole Law. (Gal. 3:10; 5:2–3)

Paul makes it clear to the Galatians that if they choose to go the way of the law, then they are under an obligation to obey every command. To break a single command is to be cursed. And there are a lot of laws to factor in. When you think you have all the laws figured out, you will discover commands you didn't even know existed, because they will come along and disqualify you. After all the effort of trying to live according to the commands of the law, you end up failing the test anyway. Legalism is truly exhausting.

When people attempt to corral behavior with rules, we soon find that we are very capable of discovering excesses to obsess about. Paul told the Galatians that the law "was added because of transgressions" (3:19). All our immoral behaviors only increase the demand for rules. He went on to say that if they tried to obey a command in order to become spiritual, then they are under obligation to obey all of them. That is quite a task.

Paul even employed some sarcasm in his attempt to correct the legalists of Galatia. As you imagine preaching Judaism to a Gentile audience, one of the first laws that would be foremost in everyone's thinking would be circumcision, especially to the men. As such, Paul often used this practice as a painful and extreme summary of all the others. To illustrate how this form of human-generated spirituality is foolish, he takes circumcision to a new level. Using the twisted logic of a legalistic approach to spirituality, Paul said: "As for those agitators [the legalists], I wish they would go the whole way and emasculate themselves!" (Gal. 5:12 NIV). In other words, why stop with the tip? If cutting off a little foreskin makes one spiritual, why not cut the whole thing off and be even more spiritual?

Jesus used similar sarcasm to address the same problem. He said, "If your right eye causes you to stumble, gouge it out and throw it away. It is better for you to lose one part of your body than for your whole body to be thrown into hell" (Matt. 5:29 NIV). Many think this addressed how serious we must take sin and to what extreme we need to go to take precautions against it. I firmly believe this was Jesus tearing down the legalistic view of the Pharisees who were listening in on the sermon. The Sermon on the Mount is a treatise against the religious rules of the Pharisees from start to finish, and it is full of humor and sarcasm if you understand its context.

It's not hard to see in this particular case. How in the world could your right eye cause you to sin but not your left eye? How would you even determine such a thing? Is it really your eye or your hand that causes sin or is it the mind that controls them? And if you followed this advice and gouged out your eyes, you would soon find that your imagination is still very capable of stumbling. What do you cut out next?

The early church preacher Origen took both Paul's and Jesus' words too literally and surgically eliminated a specific part of his body that tends to venture into the realms of sexual immorality. While recovering in his bed, he found his mind still capable of venturing into sinful realms. Too late to realize a major oops.

Taking physical actions to stop sin is not a solution to sin. We soon find that there is no end to the number of rules and regulations we can develop, and yet we will never decrease our sinfulness at all. Lists of moral restraints used by religious institutions are always being amended to include the latest fads and technological advancements. They are never satisfied, and they never work.

A quick review of Scripture discovers that the number of commands increases as humanity grows. It all started with one prohibition amid unlimited opportunity. The first man was told not to eat the fruit from one tree. That was it! Soon we find the behavior of mankind exploding with evil, and more restrictions are given. Eventually more than six hundred laws are given in the Pentateuch.

Human beings are very good at making up rules. This is job security for popes, priests, and lawyers. The church is very adept at increasing rules. A quick tour of almost any church building will reveal a lot of little signs posted throughout. For example:

- No feet on the handrail
- Flush only toilet paper in the toilet
- No running in the halls
- No bare feet in the halls or classrooms
- No loud voices in the halls
- No parking here
- No skateboards allowed
- No food or drink allowed in the sanctuary
- No cell phones allowed during the service

When something happens that we do not like, it doesn't take long for us to add a new rule to the chorus of dos and don'ts already echoing down every church hallway. The older the institution, the more rules you will find. Changing the rules or even suspending them becomes nearly impossible in some older institutions, because the people who once had the authority died a long time ago.

I was a guest lecturer at a Christian school that required two government-issued photo IDs before I could speak. I asked myself, *Is that really a big problem in the Christian school world?* After all, they had asked me to come. Surely they know who I am, right? Are there a lot of fake guest lecturers who are invited to speak and then turn out to be illegal aliens or something worse? I couldn't figure out what infraction led to such a rule, but I'm sure there was one. The Transportation Security Administration only requires one photo ID for a person to board a flight. You can enter the country with only one government-issued ID. Yet to speak at a Christian college in the Midwest, we need twice that. I made the mistake of joking about giving them a DNA sample and fingerprints. You will soon find out that the people who enforce the rules, by the very nature of their job, have no sense of humor about such things. In fact, I think that is a rule itself. Humor, like all other forms of pleasure, is against the law.

There is no ceiling for the evil we can devise, and therefore, the number of rules and restrictions are also unlimited. Every advance in technology, which is already piling up on an exponential growth curve, demands new rules to curb potential transgressions. This is exhausting and never ending.

Jesus was able to take all the commands and reduce them to just one: love God. Everything will be fulfilled if you just do that. Augustine summed it up this way: "Love God and do whatever you please." For many of us that may sound hedonistic and anarchistic. It is actually genius. It takes all the complexities of the Bible and wraps it up for us in a memorable, powerful, and concise manner. That actually is good advice, because if you really love God, you will not be pleased with anything less than being with God in everything. Augustine followed the above quote with: "for the soul trained in love to God will do nothing to offend the One who is Beloved."

In Galatians, Paul also took all the law and wrapped it up concisely when he reminded his readers: "For the whole Law is fulfilled in one word, in the statement, 'YOU SHALL LOVE YOUR NEIGHBOR AS YOURSELF'" (5:14).

Real faith is simple.

DIY spirituality, or human-generated spirituality, is complex and ever demanding. Not only are there as many rules as there are ways we can act, but we must obey each and every one of the rules to make it.

When spirituality is measured by physical appearance and observable behavior, we tend to think all is good if we meet those qualifications, but this is deluded thinking. The law demands so much more than just looking good to others. Comparison to other people actually has nothing to do with real spirituality, but it is a dominant theme in human-generated spirituality that tends to trap our minds in a deceived state.

Today's churches are under the intense weight of perfectionism as they see themselves having to compete with today's entertainment culture as well as other nearby churches. Once you start down the path of human-generated spirituality, a momentum of needing to do it better and better each time weighs heavily on the church leadership. Performances must be better than the previous week's *and* also exceed the performances of other churches competing a few blocks away.

It is an unspoken problem rampant among megachurches that a high percentage of senior pastors end up needing a forced sabbatical in order to recover from significant burnout. When you are the star that keeps the people coming and attracts new consumers, then you are always in performance mode, and what you did yesterday is not sufficient today. There is a constant demand for perfection, and such leaders are always in the spotlight.

There are a growing number of critics circling like vultures, hoping for a leader to fail, and the greater the failure, the more these scavengers feel vindicated. All of this pressure builds. Many of these leaders find themselves existing on adrenalin and caffeine, but you can only ride those ponies for a short time before they knock you out. This is not just a megachurch problem, however. Most pastors are often hovering close to burnout because they are being pulled toward the demands of consumers and constantly competing with bigger churches that have deeper pockets. The only reason this problem is perhaps more pronounced among megachurch pastors is that the demands they face are from so many people who are dependent upon them, and they tend to be the center cog in the wheel of the ministry demands. Many people's employment and job security is dependent upon the broad shoulders and demanding schedule of a celebrity pastor.

Perfection is unattainable. For this reason we quickly divert to accentuating certain things that appear attainable and ignore others that are not. This leads us to the next consequence.

3. PRIORITIES BECOME SKEWED

> *But now that you have come to know God, or rather to*
> *be known by God, how is it that you turn back again to*
> *the weak and worthless elemental things, to which you*
> *desire to be enslaved all over again? You observe days*
> *and months and seasons and years. I fear for you, that*
> *perhaps I have labored over you in vain. (Gal. 4:9–11)*

One of the problems with an external form of spirituality is that we tend to make some sins far worse than others. What is truly important gets lost in what is not of any significance at all. Usually those that are culturally more abhorrent to us become God's most despised sins, and those that are often patterns in our own lives are less of a concern to God.

I heard Mark Labberton, president of Fuller Theological Seminary, quote his father, saying, "Religion takes great things and makes them small."[1] I would add that religion takes small things and makes way too much of them.

Jesus said of the religious leaders of his day:

> Woe to you, teachers of the law and Pharisees, you hypocrites! You give a tenth of your spices—mint, dill and cumin. But you have neglected the more important matters of the law—justice, mercy and faithfulness. You should have practiced the latter, without neglecting the former. You blind guides! You strain out a gnat but swallow a camel. (Matt. 23:23–24 NIV)

Smoking is one of those cultural sins that we abhor in the US church, but actually there is no command in Scripture against it. Nevertheless, we not only forbid it but we place it among the worst sins. When we see someone with a cigarette in hand, it is assumed they are not Christians and incapable of being truly spiritual. I have found this to be far from true. Granted, smoking is an unhealthy habit that I do not recommend. But we really have to bend the Bible out of context to support our idea that it is evil and wrong.

We have many cultural sins on our list of things that cannot be compatible with Christianity, but of course the list varies with your subculture. Tattoos, cigarettes, cigars, alcohol, dancing, movies, playing cards, drums, and secular music are all on someone's list of evil practices that must be stopped if one wants to be considered spiritual. Organs were once a revolutionary new technology outlawed by many Christian churches. Today, in some churches, it is the only instrument God is capable of using. Some classic hymns are said to have used old tavern tunes with new words, which would be scandalous and controversial, to say the least. Later those same songs became the standard fare in churches that would never allow contemporary music, usually accompanied by an organ.

Once we start judging evil against good by foolish standards, all our priorities get skewed. Lesser things become worse, and the great evil the Bible actually speaks against consistently becomes allowed. In our Christian subculture we get so easily offended by minor things, while crossing lines that we never should. One particular denomination that outlaws alcohol slandered our movement because someone used something other than grape juice in communion. They never asked me (or the person who supposedly offended them) about it. Instead, they publicly denounced our entire movement as heresy, which amounts to slander. All the while they prohibited anyone from using wine in communion like Jesus and the early church did. Gossip, pride, envy, slander, and hatred are sins that are so often accepted from our pulpits and even justified as spiritual, while smoking a cigarette or having a glass of wine is demonized. Priorities are all messed up.

The Galatians' main sin priority was being uncircumcised. It became the litmus test of spirituality. Can you imagine such an environment? Suddenly, lifting up tunics to view another's private parts is considered a spiritual exercise? Women do not even merit evaluation, because they don't seem to count in what is truly spiritual. Obvious physical characteristics become the most important thing because they are observable and measurable. Soon priorities are all out of whack. Paul said, "Neither circumcision nor uncircumcision means anything, but faith working through love" (5:6). He was calling the people back to true priorities. He repeated, "For neither is circumcision anything, nor uncircumcision, but a new creation" (6:15). In the midst of busy lives, with so much going on, Paul is calling us back to a "one thing" spirituality.

Because a do-it-yourself spirituality is generated by people for people, it is ultimately subject to the opinions of people. This leads to the next consequence.

4. PLEASING OTHERS BECOMES THE RULE

For am I now seeking the favor of men, or of God? Or am I striving to please men? If I were still trying to please men, I would not be a bond-servant of Christ. . . .

For prior to the coming of certain men from James, he [Cephas/Peter] used to eat with the Gentiles; but when they came, he began to withdraw and hold himself aloof, fearing the party of the circumcision. (Gal. 1:10; 2:12)

It is a short jump from delving into a human-generated spirituality to comparing yourself with others. This is because we should be compared to the holiness of God, and by that standard we all fail. While that should push us naturally toward Christ, when we continue to value our own efforts, it quickly becomes a contest against the abilities and performances of others. Our judge is no longer God but the opinions of others (who are not shy about voicing them).

In fact, people can become the sin police and start searching for reasons to tear down others. In Galatians, Paul mentioned that false brethren came to Antioch secretly to spy and catch them in their liberty and force them into bondage (2:4). In our human-generated spiritual environment that we call church, I find that people expressing outrage or displeasure is quite common. In fact, many Christians act as if they have the spiritual gift of complaining. They see Christian leaders as called to meet their needs. And since church is where we go to be uplifted, after a while we begin to think it is all about us. We start complaining when worship isn't turning out the way we had hoped, as if the worship is for us.

This puts pressure on Christian leaders who are hired to help the church fulfill its mission. It is a short step for a Christian leader to slide from living for Jesus to living for the admiration of others.

In contrast, Paul repeatedly mentioned that he was not trying to please men but God. In fact, he usually recited the cost he paid in terms of persecution in order to continue living for Christ rather than the approval of others.

Unfortunately, when our priorities are crooked, we tend to celebrate the wrong things. We also tend to ignore the very things that are most important, which leads to the next consequence.

5. PRAISING AND MEASURING THE WRONG THINGS HIJACK OUR MISSION

*Those who desire to make a good showing in the
flesh try to compel you to be circumcised . . . so that
they may boast in your flesh. (Gal. 6:12–13)*

When external factors drive our spirituality, we are forced to measure our success against others with tangible numbers. Those who measure do-it-yourself spirituality are forced to measure it against other people to gauge their progress and determine success or failure. We do the same thing today, all the time.

The people who were leading the Galatians astray measured their success by the number of people who were captivated by their influence. They sought more and more people who could be identified as theirs, which meant they were being successful. Like spiritual scalp hunters, these legalists were measuring their success by the number of foreskins they accumulated. Paul described it, "So that they may boast in your flesh [foreskin]." While crude and ugly to us, in the midst of such deception this somehow seemed to make sense to them. I wonder what foolish things we measure today at which future generations will grimace?

Jesus spoke of this type of bad-news evangelism when he spoke of the scribes and Pharisees in this way:

> Woe to you, scribes and Pharisees, hypocrites, because you travel around on sea and land to make one proselyte; and when he becomes one, you make him twice as much a son of hell as yourselves. (Matt. 23:15)

This is not unlike our own forms of Christianity today. It is the common measure of success or failure today to measure the number of people who are attending our services. Many assume that if large numbers are coming, God is showing favor and we must be doing things right. The larger the attendance, the more successful we are thought to be. Smaller church attendance means there are problems. This type of skewed priorities and measurement causes us to celebrate people for having larger crowds. But the number of followers you have is not a measure of success; Adolf Hitler had millions of followers, whereas Jesus had twelve.

We see megachurches built on the strategy of enticing more Christians to come to their worship services and leave the churches they once were part of. Church growth has become the primary measure of success, and unfortunately what we mean by that is number of people in attendance on Sunday mornings. That is a shallow and ultimately meaningless type of measurement. So pastors spend the week trying to figure out what they can do to surpass last week's show and also compete with the show at the other church across town. Thus we've turned church into an audience at a show, not an army deployed into a hostile world with an important mission. We measure the number of people as a sure sign of success or failure, and this is completely distorted.

I found a most telling example of the arrogance of comparing ourselves with others and of measuring attendance as the standard of success in a 2012 radio interview with former megachurch pastor Mark Driscoll. He said that there was not a single decent male Bible teacher in the whole United Kingdom. Driscoll asked the host if he knew of anyone who could contradict him and then said, "You don't have one. That is a problem. There's a bunch of cowards who aren't telling the truth. . . . You don't have one young guy who can preach the Bible that anybody's listening to on the whole earth."

Of course this isn't true at all. What he was doing was using his own church and his own example as the standard of success for all other churches of the world. Any who did not compare were viewed as cowards and unsuccessful. This is the height of arrogance, and frankly I was embarrassed. Like the legalists in Galatia who were leading the early churches astray, Driscoll was measuring his success by how many followed his influence. He was holding that up as the standard by which all others should be measured.

As the conversation continued, it became apparent that the host's wife was the pastor of the church he attended. Driscoll drilled him about how many strong young men had come to Christ and attended the church, implying that they wouldn't because she was not as tough as Driscoll. The host asked him if he thought the fact that she was a woman is the reason why his church is not the same as Driscoll's church. The former megachurch pastor answered, "Yup. Yup. You look at your results, you look at my results, and you look at the variable that's most obvious."

When you are building a church based on your strengths, then you become the measure of the church's success or, as Driscoll has now discovered, its failure. Is it fair to judge one church because it's not the same as your church in Seattle? Of course not. And there are many variables besides the gender of the pastor. Mars Hill Church has gone from one of the fastest growing churches in America to one of the fastest shrinking since Driscoll has been forced to resign. I also imagine the radio host's church is doing just fine. I feel for Mark now in this difficult season and truly wish for his healing and restoration. There have been two significant moments in my own life when his messages helped me. I only use this very public example because it shows how we measure our success against others' perceived failures in a deluded manner. Hopefully we all will learn from this, including Mark.

When we measure the wrong things, we soon start to celebrate the wrong things. We also begin to discount and disrespect the right things. Jesus could draw a crowd anywhere at anytime, but he always left the crowd behind. He never trusted the false sense of success generated by having a big crowd. On the other hand, we have taken the bait and swallowed it hook, line, and sinker.

Human-generated spirituality is focused on external appearances and loses sight of what is truly important. When our spirituality is tied to pleasing people, it is not long until we start to do so at the expense of others. This sense of success at all costs leads us to the next consequence of a DIY spirituality.

6. PROLIFIC COMPETITION AND CANNIBALISM INVADE OUR CULTURE

But if you bite and devour one another, take care
that you are not consumed by one another. . . .
Let us not become boastful, challenging one
another, envying one another. (Gal. 5:15, 26)

Once we start down the path of comparing ourselves with one another for a better spiritual height, soon we find ourselves competing against one another. Paul wrote a shocking statement to the Galatians that accused them of cannibalism! But we are not far removed from that.

It is inevitable that when we start to judge our own strength against the efforts of others, tearing down others then becomes a means of personal gain. Once the success of one church is measured by the demise of another, we become a body that consumes itself. We have become cannibals for Christ. We measure our attendance against one another and fight to gain popularity as though this is a sign of success and the blessings of God, but it is not. In biology, growth that consumes the health of the body is identified as cancer and should be cut out, not celebrated.

I am amazed at how rampant and unaddressed envy is in the

church today. One thing mass public communication and social media have done is to reveal our true ugliness. We have a myriad of Christians who make it their calling to tear down others who are perceived as successful. Many rejoice when megachurch pastors fall, but I say that cannot be good.

Jealousy and envy are related spiritual distortions, but they are not the same. Jealousy is when you want what another has; envy is when you do not want what others have, but rather just don't want them to have it either. Once we start down the path of judging our spiritual success at the expense of other people, we quickly become cannibalistic Christians who devour one another. Churches are often built on the perceived failures of others, and we call that success.

In fact, the dirty little secret of most church boardrooms is that church leaders view other churches in the area as competition. It is common to have departing staff members sign a noncompete document stating they will not lead or start another church within a certain geographical distance. This is already a loss. There is no winning at this game. We all lose: pastor, staff, congregation, other churches, and those who are without Christ in the neighborhood. This is not just a bad practice, it is an aggressive cancer that must be excised immediately.

In an environment where we compete against others so that some are lifted above the rest, we naturally create a church culture that has a top-down pyramid. This leads to our next consequence.

7. PYRAMIDS OF FAME ARE BUILT

But from those who were of high reputation (what they were makes no difference to me; God shows no partiality)—well,

those who were of reputation contributed nothing to me. . . .
Recognizing the grace that had been given to me, James and
Cephas and John, who were reputed to be pillars, gave to me
and Barnabas the right hand of fellowship. (Gal. 2:6, 9)

As our spiritual culture becomes one of human performance, we soon begin to fall into ranks. Some are seen on the top of the chain of command; they become our modern-day heroes of the faith and they are seen as more spiritual than the rest. Others fall under them in various orders. Those at the very top are our celebrity pastors. Those who are not as big, famous, or well-compensated feel less than successful. The celebrity-pastor culture creates a lot of pressure to live under.

Fame itself is fickle and can be gone in a moment. It demands all your attention immediately just to keep your Klout score up and your blog traffic coming. The race to collect Twitter followers and Facebook friends is cruel and never satisfied. When your book sells well and is featured in Barnes and Noble, there is always another author's book that sold better and is featured at Walmart or Costco, upping the ante. When you are invited to speak at a conference, you feel good until you realize someone else is speaking in the prime slot and you're just a warm-up act. No matter how far up you climb the ladder of fame, there is always somebody's backside you are looking up at. Like flowing traffic on a busy four-lane freeway, fame is a race that doesn't have a finish line; it just has lots of people running and falling back—and eventually out—while younger, energetic people jump onto the track, until they, too, fall behind. No one wins this race. That is a lot of pressure to put on someone who is already busy running a church, but many are trying to do just that.

Once you are a published author or a famous speaker, there is much pressure to continue producing material to keep the success and fame going for as long as you can. Some pastors of large churches start work before the sun rises and stay busy until late at night maintaining the success of their churches. Every week another awesome sermon must be preached several times, another elder meeting must be led, another building project must be managed, another staff member must be recruited or let go. It is an unrealistic and unreasonable environment. These celebrity pastors hardly have time to write a book a year, but that is what is demanded by their success. On top of all that, after the book is written, the celebrity pastor must travel to conferences and do interviews and book-signing gigs to push the book, increasing the pressure and the demands on his or her time and health. That is why ghostwriters are hired and accusations of plagiarism increase. Some even manipulate the system to get their book atop a best-seller list.

Jesus clearly warned that this is not the way we should exist. Unfortunately it is exactly how we work. Churches become known by the name of their preacher rather than Christ's name. It becomes so easy for us to say things like, "I go to so-and-so's church." As this continues we soon find ourselves in the next consequence.

8. PASTORS BECOME IDOLS

They eagerly seek you, not commendably, but they wish to shut you out so that you will seek them. (Gal. 4:17)

It is sad but true that the natural outcome of DIY spirituality is that some people take the role of God in the lives of others. Leaders step into a place of vast importance for the life of the church. Their words become the bread of life. Granted, most would deny such a thing, but the truth is that many Christians only hear from God through the sermons of their pastors. Knowing our favorite Bible teacher's opinion on things becomes overly important to us. Many Christians are incapable of hearing from God directly and need to be told by their pastor what is right and what is wrong. God ends up having their pastor's accent.

There can only be one source of truth and life in a Christian's soul. Ours is a jealous God who will not make room for any other gods. If God's voice has your pastor's accent, it is time to repent. If your people come to you before they go to Christ, pastor, it is time to repent.

I have been to churches where everything and everyone orbits around one ego, and it isn't Christ's. If this is the climate you find yourself in, you are not going to change it unless you are the one with gravitas. A leader who feels the need to have everyone admire him and hang on his every word will not likely change because *you* don't like it. You should probably leave, because that is a toxic environment. If, however, you are the heavyweight with all the power, then you can bring change. Stop hogging all the power and start giving everything away.

But rather than correct this wrong, churches try to capitalize on it, even promoting it outright. Books are sold, podcasts are downloaded, attendance increases, and soon the preacher's status needs an insurance policy to protect the assets of the organization. The church's success is tied directly to the pastor's success, which is a precarious place to be. We start to lift our celebrity pastors up in a way no one can actually fulfill. Which leads to the next consequence.

9. PRONOUNCED HYPOCRISY IS INEVITABLE

The rest of the Jews joined him in hypocrisy, with
the result that even Barnabas was carried away
by their hypocrisy. . . . I saw that they were not
straightforward about the truth of the gospel. . . .

For those who are circumcised do not even keep
the Law themselves. (Gal. 2:13–14; 6:13)

The most prevalent accusation Christians field from the world is curiously the same in every culture of the world—hypocrisy. It is inevitable that those we lift up as idols will fail us. They will cover up their flaws for as long as possible, but eventually sin leaks.

In his book *Revangelical*, Lance Ford describes how his daughter longed to have an Apple computer to no longer have to deal with viruses and their evil twin sister—virus protection software. He saw his daughter working on her computer and thought it was at first a new Apple, but on further inspection he realized she had placed an Apple sticker on the cover of her PC laptop. She had the outward appearance of an Apple computer, but the system inside had not changed at all.[2] In a similar way, we have Christian bumper stickers and veneers on the outside that loudly and proudly proclaim we are followers of Christ, but inside there has been no transformation. We've not changed our operating system. We are hypocrites.

We mask our inadequacies with skills and rhetoric, but eventually we will be revealed as mortal and incapable of fulfilling the very spiritual standard we lift so high. Eventually entire institutions become dependent upon a single celebrity leader, and soon the entire enterprise is involved in maintaining the leader's image and brand. Many people's livelihood depends upon the continuation of the institution, so few ask critical questions and everyone contributes to the cover up, often unwittingly so.

All this results in a spirituality that looks Christian on the outside but is empty on the inside. That is the very definition of hypocrisy. The world sees it and rejects it.

In his book *The Evangelicals You Don't Know*, Tom Krattenmaker points out, "In 2008, when 'enhanced interrogation' stood center stage in the headlines . . . 57% of white evangelical Christians in the South believed torture could be justified, in contrast to the 48% of the general public."[3] As we continue down the paths of do-it-yourself spirituality that is disengaged from the true spirit and teachings of Jesus, we find that our lives look less like Jesus' than those who do not even claim Christ. Krattenmaker goes on to show that once the survey was tweaked a bit, and those taking the survey were challenged to view the subject with the Bible in mind, particularly the phrase "do unto others as you would have them do unto you," the percentage that agreed that torture was wrong rose to a slight majority.[4]

We are not "straightforward about the truth of the gospel," and everyone but us knows it. Most people can smell hypocrisy almost immediately, though proving it sometimes takes a bit longer. We must clean up our lives on the inside if we ever want people to desire what we have. Until then, we will see an ever-increasing apathy toward our message that will become outright hostile and unapologetically so.

A Christianity that is only Christian in outward appearance has nothing but rot on the inside. When enough people are singing the same tune, all of Christianity is reduced to an empty shell without any real life within. Christianity without Christ is an awful thing. That is the final consequence.

10. PRACTICING CHRISTIANITY WITHOUT CHRIST BECOMES NORMAL

I am amazed that you are so quickly deserting Him who called you by the grace of Christ, for a different gospel; which is really not another; only there are some who are disturbing you and want to distort the gospel of Christ. . . .

I do not nullify the grace of God, for if righteousness comes through the Law, then Christ died needlessly. . . .

Behold I, Paul, say to you that if you receive circumcision, Christ will be of no benefit to you. . . . You have been severed from Christ, you who are seeking to be justified by law; you have fallen from grace. (Gal. 1:6–7; 2:21; 5:2, 4)

The worst consequence of all when we choose do-it-yourself spirituality is that we get what we wanted—a Christianity all on our own. Our message becomes null and void. We are deserting Christ and making his message meaningless. Soon the world can no longer hear what we say because our lives are too unsavory. We are an empty shell of Christianity, void of the real Christ.

Nearly 80 percent of the US population call themselves Christian, but there is so little of Jesus seen in our nation.[5] It is estimated that as many as 50 percent of those who "make decisions for Christ" do not actually follow Christ in their lives.[6] What do we do with that?

If many of the people in our churches are not followers of Christ, how do we manage their spiritual lives? It is no wonder that we resort to external behavior modification techniques to keep churchgoers in line. We resort to a false gospel of do-it-yourself Christianity with rules, bylaws, and bumper-sticker slogans because it is all we can do with a populace that lacks a true gospel transformation within. A people who are not regenerate and without the indwelling Spirit are incapable of living out a truly godly life. That is true whether those people attend church or not. Preaching messages at them and forming accountability for behavior will not make them any more spiritual.

We are in a "chicken and egg" situation. It is hard to find out which came first. Is it this way because we do not preach the true gospel or do we preach a false gospel because we are dealing with this sort of congregation? The solution is the same in either case: embrace and live out the true gospel. We must be born again: redeemed, regenerated, and filled with the Holy Spirit. We must experience a true change from the inside out by the power of Christ's presence. That is the only solution, period.

Those who troubled the Galatians came to "distort the gospel of Christ" (1:7). That is perhaps the worst consequence of human-generated spirituality. We become so content with a false gospel that we have no clue what the real thing is.

When we become so accustomed to the type of goodness that is only possible by humans, we have no imagination for a goodness that is possible only by God. As a result, we often see those without the Spirit of God actually doing better and looking more loving than those who supposedly have the Holy Spirit. This dumbing down of love is evident in our churches to such an extent that none are attracted to us but are actually, in many cases, repelled by us.

Tim Keller hit on this when he said, "Revival occurs when those who think they already know the gospel discover they do not really or fully know it."[7] That is a revolution.

Like the proverbial frog in the pot of water that slowly heats to a boil, we are not actually aware of how hot the water is. We are tempted to say things like, "It can't be all that bad. Look at all the good things our churches are doing." But the Galatians were very good when compared against human standards seen in other people and churches. But is that really what we want? Is that what Christ came for? Are we really going to be satisfied with less than the whole presence of Christ living in and through us and instead become content with good sermons, hot music, laser beams, fog machines, and celebrity pastors?

To review, below are the ten consequences of do-it-yourself spirituality that the Galatians suffered from and I believe we still do today:

1. Pride and self-deception start us down the wrong path. (Gal. 6:3, 7)
2. Perfection drives us . . . or all is lost. (Gal. 3:10; 5:2–3)
3. Priorities become skewed. (Gal. 4:9–11)
4. Pleasing others becomes the rule. (Gal. 1:10; 2:12)
5. Praising and measuring the wrong things hijack our mission. (Gal. 6:12–13)
6. Prolific competition and cannibalism invade our culture. (Gal. 5:15, 26)
7. Pyramids of fame are built. (Gal. 2:6, 9)
8. Pastors become idols. (Gal. 4:17)

9. Pronounced hypocrisy is inevitable. (Gal. 2:13–14; 6:13)
10. Practicing Christianity without Christ becomes normal.
    (Gal. 1:6–7; 2:21; 5:2, 4)

I suggest you take a moment and pray. Humbly ask God to open your eyes to the true state of your spirituality for a moment. Read through the list above, asking God to reveal any way that you have been deceived and may be promulgating these problems in your church. This takes courage and honesty. You must be vulnerable and authentic. Otherwise you will suffer all of the above and not even know it.

The alternative to courageous and vulnerable honesty is defensiveness and reactions against problems that will set you back on your heels constantly and drive you to places you do not want to be. That is our enemy's strategy and it is all too often effective. The next chapter will address how this strategy has stolen so much of our vital Christian life.

Chapter 3

REVOLUTIONS ARE NEVER WON ON DEFENSE

*If you want others to be more loving, choose
to love first. If you want a reconciled outer
world, reconcile your own inner world.*
—RICHARD ROHR

Be the change you wish to see in the world.
—MOHANDAS GANDHI

There was no question about it. In 1980 the Soviet Union's
national hockey team was the best in the world. No one else
could compete with them, not even the professionals in the NHL.

Going into the 1980 Winter Olympics, no one expected anyone but the Soviets would win the gold medal. In fact, it was such a
sure thing that when the US hockey team defeated them and went
on to win the gold medal, their victory was called a *miracle.*

In the Disney film about the matchup between the Soviet
and American teams, titled *The Miracle*, Kurt Russell, portray-
ing coach Herb Brooks, shows the young men films of the Soviets

running circles around their opponents. They had even beaten an all-star-filled NHL team. After shutting down the films, Brooks turns to his players and gives them a short, inspiring speech that reveals the secret to defeating this Goliath.

"Their main weapon is intimidation. They know they're gonna win, and so do their opponents."

He then dropped his head and said with brutal honesty, "Look, I can give you all a load of crap about how you're a better team than they are, but that's exactly what it'd be. And everyone in this room knows what people say about our chances. I know it. You know it."

With every face looking blank at a pep talk that was anything but encouraging, Brooks said, "But I also know there is a way to stay with this team."

At this point, he crossed out a whole lot of *x*'s and *o*'s on the chalkboard and said, "You don't *defend* them."

He then drew a long, straight arrow in the opposite direction and said, "You *attack* them! You take their game and you shove it right back in their face. The team that is finally willing to do this is the team that has a chance to put them down. NHL won't change their game. We will. The rest of the world is afraid of them. Boys, we won't be."

We know this team of amateur players, with few real superstars at all, went on to defeat the Soviets and win a gold medal. They pulled off a miracle.

Revolutions are never won on defense. Only in the NFL can the defense score points. As long as the church is on its heels, we will continue to lose ground. We must stop being so defensive and start countering the world system with a more proactive and positive strength. We must take the gospel as our strength and power and reengage the world, believing this will work. Our ambition must not be to keep what we have or defend what we were; we must not be content with anything less than changing the world for the better. The high cost of the gospel itself deserves it. No! It *demands* nothing less.

A PROACTIVE—NOT REACTIVE—CHURCH

According to Stephen Covey, one of the seven habits of highly effective people is the ability to be proactive rather than simply reactive to outside influences.[1] When we react to whatever is occurring around us, we surrender our lives to forces that are neutral at best but often are maleficent. We allow external forces to define the most important questions of life, such as who are we and what are we about. Identity and mission are two core elements of existence that should not be sacrificed to the impulse of outside forces.

When we are simply reactive, we are allowing others to determine our agenda and our own actions, and we surrender the power necessary to truly change things. This is because we are allowing external forces to determine our limits, our activities, and how we relate in them.

Proactive people are not defined by what is outside. They assert influence over what is outside of them based on who they are and what they perceive as their mission. What is inside of them affects what is outside of them, not the other way around. They turn the tables so external forces, whatever they may be, must react to their identity and mission. This is a revolutionary power, and it results in a more real and longer-lasting change. Reactive people simply make excuses based on what is happening to them and allow external elements to define them.

This is not how Jesus saw his church. In Matthew 16:18 he said, "Upon this rock I will build My church; and the gates of Hades will not overpower it." In my book *Organic Church*, I pointed out that gates are not defensive weapons.[2] Police don't carry loaded gates. Terrorists don't hold people at gate point. Dogs don't wear signs that say Beware of Gate. A gate is defensive, and the gates of hell itself cannot stop the church that Jesus builds. Jesus saw his church on offense, proactive and demanding that hell alter its agenda because of us, not the other way around.

In his letter to the Galatians, Paul challenged his readers to turn from defense to offense. We need to shift our weight from our heels to our toes and push the darkness back on its heels. The gospel that sets us free establishes us in a proactive role in life rather than simply deferring to the impulse of the other side. The apostle said:

> For you were called to freedom, brethren; only do not turn your freedom into an opportunity for the flesh, but through love serve one another. . . .
>
> But I say, walk by the Spirit, and you will not carry out the desire of the flesh. For the flesh sets its desire against the Spirit, and the Spirit against the flesh; for these are in opposition to one another, so that you may not do the things that you please. But if you are led by the Spirit, you are not under the Law. (Gal. 5:13, 16–18)

Unfortunately the church in general has been reactive for a long, long time. Whatever raises its head up in this world, the church takes a stand against and reacts to it. By doing this we forfeit our mission to the whims of whatever comes along. We have actually allowed these external influences to define who we are. In fact, our very beginning is defined by a reaction to what was happening at that time. Most of us are known as Protestants. We are known as those who *protest* against what is occurring. This is a very reactive form of identity. From our very start we have been reactionary. We are most known for what we are not, and it is time to be known for the freedom that we are for.

Reaction is very limited in the kind of impact it has on the world. The reason for this is that it starts and ends with the activity of an external force rather than a strong sense of personal identity and mission. A reactive thought process allows the external threat (whatever it is) to define the conversation and objectives.

One of the most devastating effects of being only reactive, which is often not recognized, is that it forfeits something important about its own identity and mission with a narrow focus on defining itself as being "not something."

In this chapter, I illustrate how this has happened time and again in church history. From the Reformation until now, we have allowed our reaction to others to determine who we are or are not. In so doing we have also forfeited a part of our own being that should never have been lost. I will show how our reactions to three different forces have caused us to lose two very important elements in each case, affecting both our identity and mission. As a result, we are less than we should be.

REACTIONS TO ROMAN CATHOLICISM

In many ways, our whole identity was formed by our reaction against something. As Protestants, we were birthed as reactionary, and so our entire makeup is inclined this way. In a way, our sense of identity is that we are not Catholic. Perhaps our DNA is set as reactionary.

The very first force we reacted against was Roman Catholicism. There could likely be volumes of scholarly writings about how this reaction defined us. I want to identify only two important elements that should be part of the fabric of our life that was forfeited simply in reaction against something we viewed as wrong.

While Martin Luther's ninety-five theses were nailed to the Wittenberg church door and launched the Reformation, the most pressing doctrine that we reacted against was the selling of indulgences by the church. But there were two things we lost in our reaction against Catholicism that affected us the most: (1) we rejected the apostolic gift and lost the foundations of movements, and (2) we rejected the confession of sin and lost a vital spiritual life.

The Apostolic Gift and the Foundations of Movements

Long ago we reacted against papal authority and succession. Protestants rejected apostolic succession, and in many ways this is right. We should not have a pope. There is only one mediator between God and us, and that is Jesus. But in our zeal to reject the Roman Catholic doctrine of apostolic succession, we unfortunately also rejected the apostolic gift entirely. The result is that we sacrificed our apostolic foundations.

We should have rejected the hierarchical worldview that enabled such papal abuses, but instead we rejected the entire apostolic role. We kept the hierarchical view, and to this day we remain under the lie that the clergy are responsible to God for the rest of us. What we rejected was the importance of apostles among us, and we kept the same abusive chain-of-command structures that we hated. While shouting "There is only one mediator between God and people," we maintained a clergy and laity structure that was born to replace Christ as *the* mediator. This illustrates how a foolish reactionary response to external forces tricks us and steals from us, because it takes us away from our core bearings.

Roman Catholics point to Matthew 16:18, where the Lord said to Peter that he would build his church on a strong foundation, to defend the doctrine of apostolic and papal succession. He then gave Peter the keys to the kingdom. Catholics argue that the church's foundation is the rock, namely, Peter. Protestants argue that Peter's statement in Matthew 16:16 ("You are the Christ, the Son of the living God") indicates that Christ is the foundation of the church. Either interpretation can be defended, though I actually think the Catholic argument is slightly stronger in view of the entirety of the New Testament. That said, I believe the application of their interpretation is far off base.

But in our zeal to be anti-Catholic, we refused to accept that Peter could in any way be foundational to the church that Jesus was building. But this isn't in accord with the rest of the New Testament, which clearly teaches that apostles and prophets are indeed the foundation of the church (Rom. 15:20; 1 Cor. 3:10–12; Eph. 2:20). Instead, we threw the apostles under the bus and built our churches on the foundations of local pastors and teachers. As a result, we are not the movement we were meant to be. It is the apostolic gift that empowers ordinary Christ followers, and multiplication occurs as a result. Remove apostolic influences, and rapid multiplication is lost and Christianity is replaced with centralized teaching institutions.[3]

False apostles, according to the New Testament, desire to sit atop the chain of command in a place of honor, worthy of salary, and must project a larger-than-life charismatic personality. These counterfeits actually steal the true gift from us, and this is why Paul had to deal so strongly against these false apostles who proclaimed that he wasn't a real apostle. Even today we are fighting against counterfeit apostolic expressions, not just with the pope, but in many other circles as well.

Paul called counterfeit apostles "superapostles" (2 Cor. 11:13–14). In most English Bibles, this is translated as "false apostles"; the actual term is *(h)uper-apostolos*, which can also be translated as "superapostle" or "überapostle." But Paul was mocking these men who aspire to be outstanding among all the ordinary people. These were not true apostles, but counterfeits. And the counterfeits were designed by our enemy to be shiny and larger than life. Paul wrote:

> For such men are false [super] apostles, deceitful workers, disguising themselves as apostles of Christ. No wonder, for even Satan disguises himself as an angel of light. Therefore it is not surprising if his servants also disguise themselves as servants of righteousness, whose end will be according to their deeds. (2 Cor. 11:13–15)

Superapostles strove to be greater than all others. Their spirit was not the humble spirit of Christ, which was generous and uplifting of others (2 Cor. 11:20–21). If true apostles were the custodians of the gospel, false apostles corrupted the gospel and made it about something else (2 Cor. 11:4). They emphasized their apostolic power and authority and demanded greater financial rewards for it (2 Cor. 11:7–13). They pointed to themselves as the ones with the most dramatic and charismatic personalities and defamed Paul for being less charismatic in person than in writing and not as good a communicator as they were (2 Cor.11:5–6). They did not emphasize the *releasing* of power for others but rather focused on their own empowerment. It is remarkable how close some of the literature about apostles today comes to Paul's description of the false superapostles.[4]

It looks as though we let the false apostles win because we have chosen no apostles rather than just deal with the false ones. Our reactive nature has allowed the Enemy to steal something of utmost importance. We must be careful not to toss aside a needed gift because we reject a counterfeit expression of it.

Is it possible to allow for Peter to be a foundation for the church without succumbing to papal succession? Of course it is. Peter was an apostle; you might even argue he was the first apostle. And the apostles were the foundation of the church. But does that mean that any other apostles to come are above all others? No. In fact, it doesn't even mean that Peter was above all others among his peers. Paul addressed that fully in Galatians when he mentioned that he visited the apostles in Jerusalem. He called them pillars of the church and men of high reputation, but then he added that they were nothing to him, because God is not a respecter of persons. He recounted how he confronted Peter himself in front of everyone at Antioch (Gal. 2:1–21).

Paul later described himself as the "least of the apostles" (1 Cor. 15:9). Nevertheless, he said that he was in no way "inferior to the most eminent apostles" (2 Cor. 11:5). Reading these words with a hierarchical lens makes it difficult to understand, but in truth it is not far from how Jesus described leadership in his kingdom: "The last shall be first, and the first last" (Matt. 20:16). In a race, if the person who comes in last also comes in first, and the one who comes in first also comes in last, what do you have?

There is a simple answer to this riddle. You have a tie. That is the ranking in Jesus' kingdom—we are all tied for first and last place. There is not one above another, but all are equal and all are under the headship of Christ.

In the world you have a hierarchy where some are higher and more important and powerful than others. That is the way of the world. But Jesus said, "It is not this way among you" (Matt. 20:26).

It isn't the word *apostle* that is troublesome. It isn't even the role or function that is a problem. The true problem is a hierarchical pyramid of power that puts others between God and his people, and ironically, in all our reactions to the errors of Catholicism, that's the one thing we didn't reject.

Confession and a Vital Spiritual Life

A second thing we rejected because of the rejection of any other mediator besides Christ was the confessional. This, of course, makes sense if you are just thinking about a box where a parishioner confesses to a priest, who then prescribes some penitent actions to confessors and grants forgiveness. We should reject that. But unfortunately we went too far and rejected confession to anyone other than God.

Are we to verbally confess our sins to priests? Yes, actually we are, because we are all priests, and we are to confess to one another. But because of our reaction against Catholicism, we abandoned this idea.

This is a serious issue because we truly cannot have a vital spiritual community without mutual confession. We cite 1 John 1:9 as proof that we need only confess to God, but the context of that verse is clearly confession before others. That very passage indicates that we are not to be trusted if we do not acknowledge our sin before others. Cleansing, forgiveness, and healing are the fruits of confession to one another.

Consequently, the world sees us as judgmental hypocrites because we point out everyone else's sin and refuse to acknowledge our own. In large part the world is right. If we would open up and be real, authentic, and vulnerable before others, we would immediately disarm the world.

REACTIONS TO LIBERALISM

Near the beginning of the last century there was a humanistic worldview that spread like a virus from Germany and Europe to all over the Western world. It rejected the Scriptures as inspired truth from God. The so-called enlightened view of higher criticism, labeled as liberalism, was countered by those who held to the fundamentals of the faith and produced a series of books called *The Fundamentals*.[5] Those who stood against liberalism became known as fundamentalists. Today, *fundamentalist* is often applied to anyone so narrow-minded that they can peer through a keyhole with both eyes at the same time. But it wasn't always that way. There is beauty and power in the simple fundamentals of our faith.

In our reaction to liberalism, two core missional identities were sacrificed with devastating effects: (1) we rejected ministry to the poor and social justice, and (2) we rejected unity among the churches.

Ministry to the Poor and Social Justice

Void of the absolute truth found in Scripture and yet needing a reason to exist as a religious institution, most liberal churches found an outlet in serving the poor and trying to overthrow injustices. This allowed them to remain spiritual and yet still able to reject the basic tenets of the gospel. Liberation theology arose in Latin America and fueled revolutions on behalf of the oppressed.

The church reacted against liberal forces by rejecting some of its tenets. Of course, first and foremost, the church rejected the view that Scripture is not authoritative but rather is inspired by God and inerrant in its original documents. But, unfortunately, we also found it expedient to reject the call to help the poor and follow through on social justice initiatives. We called this misbegotten theology a "social gospel," devoid of the real gospel. There may be some truth to this. However, the New Testament describes the mission of Christ this way:

> And He [Jesus] opened the book and found the place
>> where it was written,
> "The Spirit of the Lord is upon Me,
> Because He anointed Me to preach the gospel to the poor.
> He has sent Me to proclaim release to the captives,
> And recovery of sight to the blind,
> To set free those who are oppressed,
> To proclaim the favorable year of the Lord." (Luke 4:17–19)

There is no doubt that part of the gospel is about setting captives free and doing good for the poor. In fact, there is probably no designation of people that we are commanded to care for more than the poor. Just a survey of the wisdom found in the book of Proverbs reveals God's concern for the poor and how we are to share that concern (14:21, 31; 17:5; 19:17; 21:13; 28:27; 29:7, 14). God has chosen the poor to be rich in faith (James 2:5), and most revivals and multiplying movements of the gospel tend to start among the poor. Jesus' condemnation of the Pharisees was partly because they neglected the issue of justice for those who were oppressed: "But woe to you Pharisees! For you pay tithe of mint and rue and every kind of garden herb, and yet disregard justice and the love of God" (Luke 11:42).

While a social gospel is not the whole gospel, it certainly is part of it. What concerns me most is that the gospel we preach is not the whole gospel either, and we see so little results because of it.

For most of the church, the gospel has been reduced to evangelism with a message about going to heaven after death. While that is part of the gospel, it is not the whole message. Ironically, while accusing others of shortchanging the gospel, this seems to be the very thing we have done ourselves in our reaction to the social gospel. Even to this day, if you have a passion for social issues, you will be held very suspect by a great many people in the church.

There is an irony in our holding so tightly to the Scriptures in this battle but not listening to them when they command us to care for the poor and oppressed. If we are not willing to obey them, why do we fight so hard to keep them?

Unity Among the Churches

While it may sound harsh to claim such a thing, a simple observance of our hundreds of schisms, denominations, and organizations that do not play well together reveals how much we have rejected unity among the churches. There are probably many reasons for this, but one clear reason is our reaction against liberals and anything ecumenical.

Many well-established organizations fell to liberalism. It may surprise you to hear that Harvard, Yale, and many elite colleges were originally established to train pastors in theology. Some of the best academic institutions became liberal bastions. Watching this happen time and again, many evangelical denominations and churches began to fear the encroachment of liberalism. They reacted against it by avoiding those who were different doctrinally.

The World Council of Churches started out well, but over time the organization became a liberal group. This caused a reaction in the conservative evangelical wing of the church. A fear arose that if we rubbed shoulders with people from other denominations and doctrines, we might compromise and lose our solid beliefs. Of course, if they were really that solid, there shouldn't be such a fear. As a result of this fear, anything that hinted of ecumenism was considered liberal and avoided. In some circles, even the word *ecumenical* became synonymous with liberalism.

The irony is that the Bible these pastors fought so hard for is very clear that being united is very important, in many cases it is more important than being right on several issues. In fact, one can argue that divisiveness is a false doctrine that the Bible clearly denounces. We cannot display the love of God in an unloving way. The world sees our divisiveness and is not attracted by it. We must ask the following question: Can we be united and not lose our core doctrinal distinctives? I believe this is not only possible but preferable. We must learn to celebrate the diversity in Christ's body and learn from one another while not abandoning the very truth that gives us life.

REACTIONS TO CULTS

Cults have long been at the top of the chart of things we should be concerned about. Entire ministries are built on the idea of exposing cults or helping people escape from them. Whenever I speak about spontaneous expansion of the organic church, I get the same question: How will you keep cults from sprouting up everywhere?[6] We have been conditioned to think that this is a very big concern. It is not.

I will ask an audience to raise their hand if they ever met someone who started a cult. Usually, at most, two hands in a good-sized room will go up. Then I'll ask them to raise their hand if they ever knew a Christian leader who fell into immorality. Almost everyone raises their hand. I will follow this up by saying, "I don't think cults are our biggest concern."

Jesus said we would always have false teaching among us, so I decided a long time ago that I would stop trying to eliminate something that Jesus said would not be eliminated. My life got much simpler. My aim is to teach what is true and not try to discover and attack all that is untrue. We must become proactive rather than reactive. But there are two things we rejected that we shouldn't have: (1) we rejected God's voice outside of a hermeneutic of Scripture, and (2) we rejected marginalization in our world.

God's Voice Outside of Scripture

With the rise of cults like Jehovah's Witnesses and Mormons, one of the things we reacted against was that people could write new Scripture. This is something we should be wary of, but in our reaction, we lost something else. A sound interpretation of the Scriptures became the only way God could speak to us. We muzzled God for fear that giving permission for just anybody to hear from God would result in rampant cults.

With this reaction we lost perhaps the most important and powerful resource we have: the voice of our Shepherd. Don't get me wrong; I know Jesus speaks through the Scripture. But there is also an imminence that is vital and powerful that we lost.

But even his voice in the Scriptures itself was threatened, because we didn't trust just anyone to read and interpret the Scriptures correctly. We only trusted trained professionals who had the correct hermeneutic to understand the Scriptures. With time, even the Scriptures were lost to many believers, who could only hear God through their pastors' sermons.

I have written extensively about this very idea,[7] so I will not go much further here. The New Testament indicates, however, that you can identify the real sons and daughters of King Jesus and who are not by whether or not they hear God's voice (John 10:3–5, 27; Rom. 8:14; Gal. 5:16–24). In light of our reactions against cults and our restrictions with the voice of God and even the Bible itself, we should all be very concerned about this.

Marginalization in Our World

Cults are a big deal in church, but not just in church. All over the world we find that cults are considered evil and sinister movements in society. They have fostered a fear of anything that is not like an institutional church. All over Europe, Christians are fearful of being labeled a sect or cult by a government. In many nations there is a state church, and anything else is not to be trusted. Anything that looks different from the church of their great-great-grandparents is suspected of being a cult.

I have found that missionaries are afraid of being labeled a cult because that would cause the people of that nation to fear them and never listen to what they have to say. Should we react in fear this way? No. Every good work of God was once labeled a cult.

I tell people to imagine placing all the Christians who ever lived in one room, and then divide that room into two halves, with, on one side, all those who were labeled orthodox by their peers and, on the other side, those who were labeled heretical by their peers. I ask them, "Which side of the room would you rather be found in?" On the side with orthodox people are names and faces you have never seen or heard. On the heretical side you will find all your heroes, including the apostle Paul, Martin Luther, John Wesley, and even Jesus himself. I've said to missionaries afraid of being labeled a cult that they should not be afraid. In fact, they should be afraid of not being called a cult. If a world system under the control of the god of this world thinks you are doing things right, *then* you should be afraid.

There are memorable moments when a single decision made all the difference in the outcome of our lives. Some for the better, some not. One such moment for me was in 1998. I was asked to lead the church planting efforts for my denomination in Southern California and was invited to a retreat with executives from the other denominations in our area. All of us were church planting and expansion experts. My feelings shifted, however, when I drove to the meeting. I went from being excited to be a part of such an important meeting to being disappointed for thinking that way. Why? I realized it was hard to think that a single meeting would ever change the world. Meetings like the one I would be attending happen all the time all over the world. They feel important, and the attendees think they are historic, but they never actually change much of anything. It is always the folks in the margins of life who ignite real change.

I left that meeting determined to never become a denominational executive. I would start a church myself and I would do so on the streets. A couple of years later, Awakening Chapels began among a very ostracized group that would never darken the doorway of a typical church. Organic church movements were ignited.

The people in the margins are not to be avoided, because that is the field of our greatest influence. You will be hard-pressed to find many examples of the church making a huge difference in the mainstream of any culture, but most revivals and movements are born out on the margins. We should not fear being marginalized; we should fear being mainstreamed. That has always led to the downfall of our faith.

These observations are brief and broad. I understand this is not an in-depth analysis, for that is not the intent of this book. My objective is merely to point out some of what we have lost of our identity and mission as a spiritual movement because we reacted against something rather than proactively pursuing our core mission from a secure sense of identity.

A reactionary stance that forfeits all initiative to outside forces will forever be on the defense and never advance the real cause. To really impact our world, we must have a fire burning within that is contagious. In the next chapter I will examine this internal drive that can spread from life to life.

Chapter 4

LIGHTING THE FIRES
OF REVOLUTION

*A fundamental mistake of the conservative side
of the American church today, and much of the
Western church, is that it aims to get people into
heaven rather than to get heaven into people.*
—DALLAS WILLARD

*Free will, though it makes evil possible, is
also the only thing that makes possible any
love or goodness or joy worth having.*
—C. S. LEWIS

There is an old story told of a Native American chief who had become a Christian. He was asked by the missionary that discipled him what it felt like now that he was a Christian.

The chief answered, "It is like I have two big dogs fighting inside of me. One is a white dog and the other a black dog."

Instantly, the missionary knew what the chief was describing, because it is a tension we all feel within. Since he wanted the new disciple to have an assurance of his salvation, the missionary asked, "So which dog do you think will win?"

After a pause, the chief said, "Whichever I feed the most."

There is a battle within us. There are two ways before us, and they are not complementary in any way but are eternally opposed to one another. They will lead us to either destruction or eternal life, but you cannot feed them both. You can only feed one.

The battle in this world is won or lost inside each of us. We cannot hope to make a difference on the outside if we are not different on the inside. As my ministry partner Dezi Baker would say, "We must be different enough to make a difference in a very different world." If we are the same as everyone else, we have nothing to offer the world.

TWO WAYS, ONE CHOICE

An invisible line stretches from Mount Seward in Alaska through North America, Central America, and South America, all the way to the tip of the cape in Argentina. It is called the Continental Divide. When it rains on the top of a mountain along the Continental Divide, the water can flow either east or west. Two drops of rain that hit the ground simultaneously within inches of each other can flow in different directions and follow paths to oceans separated by an entire continent. That is why it is called the Continental Divide. The water from one drop could end up in the Atlantic Ocean and the Pacific.

In a similar way we each face two different paths that lead to completely opposite destinations. You cannot get to one destination by following the other path. And while we face two paths, we are only allowed one choice.

ONE THING

Paul stated boldly, "The flesh sets its desire against the Spirit, and the Spirit against the flesh; for these are in opposition to one another, so that you may not do the things that you please. But if you are led by the Spirit, you are not under the Law" (Gal. 5:17–18).

We are facing two paths and the destinations of each could not be farther apart than heaven and hell. One path is the path of doing good (the flesh). The other is the path of grace (the Spirit) because you are not good without it.

Christianity is dominated by a pragmatic spirit that will accept whatever seems to work. If it does good, it can't be all that bad, right? We are tempted to believe that any good that is done can only be helpful to the cause. If what we are doing is good, how can it be bad? Why can't we accept both kinds of good? Is the reason why we do good really all that important as long as good is done?

Our problem is that we think the way to our desired destination is to take the opposite path. You can't. You cannot get to Los Angeles by taking the road to New York. A do-it-yourself spirituality cannot be thought of as neutral or tolerable in any way. So when you are feeding the flesh, you are, according to Scripture, rejecting and quenching the Spirit. Even if what you are doing looks good and sounds good in the eyes of everyone around you, if it is not from the Spirit, it is against the Spirit. This is not neutral.

Paul laid out for us a contrast of the deeds of the flesh versus the fruit of the Spirit. Here we find indicators of authentic or counterfeit spirituality.

It is quite common to watch celebrity preachers and notice

that the ministry environment orbiting around them has more in common with the deeds of the flesh than with the fruit of the Spirit. The deeds of the flesh include "enmities, strife, jealousy, outbursts of anger, disputes, dissensions, factions, envying" (Gal. 5:20–21). It is actually quite common to see these on display from pulpits across America. Paul mentioned that the deeds of the flesh (DIY spirituality) "are evident." I would add that the evidence is prolific and, unfortunately, way too acceptable in our spiritual climate today. We have been deluded to the point that often we see these deeds as not only acceptable but even godly endeavors.

You cannot get the fruit of the Spirit (Gal. 5:22–23) by practicing the deeds of the flesh (5:19–21). The two paths are diametrically opposed. That is why we cannot be content with good works that are done in the flesh. Frankly, this is why I am writing this book. We have become too accepting of a counterfeit spirituality that results in pride and delusional thinking. This must end if we have any hope of truly making a difference in this world.

We have been far too tolerant and accepting of activities of the flesh. According to Paul's words in Galatians, we are not just to deny the flesh, we are to crucify it (5:24). Let that sink in a moment. There can hardly be any form of execution more horrifying than crucifixion. The Roman statesman and philosopher Cicero called it "a most cruel and disgusting punishment."

The flesh is not to be tolerated, excused, toyed with, allowed, ignored, or overlooked. It is to be seized by force, brought to submission, and then dragged to a violent and humiliating death—nailed alive to a cross until it stops breathing. This is not something we can mix in with some of the Spirit. The flesh is our enemy, not our friend. It is against God in every way, and we cannot use it for God.

The flesh is me. I am to execute myself in a horrifying and violent manner. That is the only way Christ can live in and through me. Paul writes:

> I have been crucified with Christ; and it is no longer I who live, but Christ lives in me; and the life which I now live in the flesh I live by faith in the Son of God, who loved me and gave Himself up for me. (Gal. 2:20)

Writing to the Philippians, likely against the same legalists, Paul says, "For we are the true circumcision, who worship in the Spirit of God and glory in Christ Jesus and put no confidence in the flesh" (3:3).

Whenever I use some hand sanitizer, I notice the label boasts that it kills 99.9 percent of germs. I always smile when I read that. While the label is meant to be a comfort to us because it means this stuff really works, my thoughts are always drawn to that 0.01 percent germ. That must be a strong germ, a super bacteria that can outlive a nuclear holocaust of Purell. If so, it would likely be the one to kill me—kill all of us for that matter. It only takes one apocalyptic germ to destroy us all.

Paul says we are to put zero confidence in the flesh. Not even 0.01 percent. If we put even that little confidence in the flesh, we are not operating in the Spirit at all. So much of what the church does is powered in the flesh. So much of what I do is fueled by the flesh. All of that is worthless. Crucify it. As long as we operate in the flesh we are not operating in the Spirit. This is all or nothing.

MOTIVES MAKE A DIFFERENCE

Motives are important. What gets you up in the morning and what keeps you up late at night says a lot about you. Most people in the world have screwed-up motivations. Let's face it, we all grew up in some form of dysfunction, and we have allowed those scars to identify us in some rather deep and lasting ways. We can and should change, but it requires that we stop feeding the wrong motives and start feeding the right ones. We simply cannot find health by fueling the things that make us unhealthy.

Internal Versus External Motivations

There are different kinds of motivations. External motivations have a source outside of us; whereas, internal motivations rise from within us. The old proverb differentiates these motivations: "You can lead a horse to water, but you can't make him drink." Another well-known example that also touches on external and internal motivations (and also employs the equine analogy) is the idea of using a carrot on a stick (internal) or a stick on the backside (external) to motivate a horse.

Both kinds of motivations can be effective. We can get results with either external or internal motivations. In fact, sometimes external motivations are the only way to get things done.

Internal motivations come from within us. This excludes any other person as a motivational source. Internal motivations are, for that reason, stronger, but they also take any management and control out of the hands of others.

Natural Versus Spiritual Motivations

Some motivations are natural, meaning they are shared universally by all people—past, present, or future. Some are more ethereal or spiritual motivations that are options to everyone but motivate us only if we choose to let them. These are chosen motivations, whether the source comes from within or without.

Both natural and spiritual motivations are universal. The difference is that one set requires a choice and the other is so much a part of being human that you cannot exist without it. Consequently everyone on the planet is constantly experiencing natural motivations, but not everyone is moved by spiritual motivations.

If we lay these four different motivational factors on a chart, mapping out the possible configurations, it would look like the diagram below, where the internal is opposite the external and the natural is opposite the spiritual.[1]

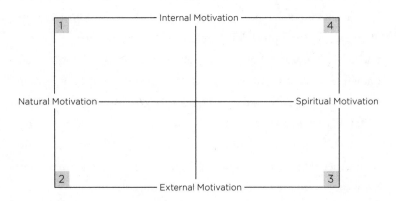

This gives us four quadrants of motivation, where internal and external motivations overlap with natural and spiritual motivations.

In the upper left (Quadrant 1) a person is motivated internally in a natural way, the same as everyone on the planet. Our identity, pride, and pleasures fall into this quadrant of motivation.

In the bottom left (Quadrant 2) we find natural external motivations, which are applied all around the world to get people to

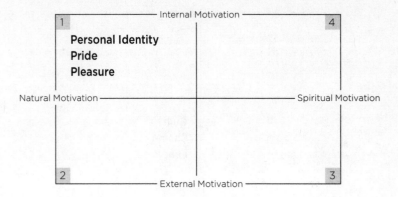

do what others want. In all cultures and nations, people use the threat of pain, peer pressure, and paychecks to get people to do what they want.

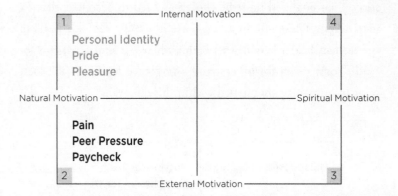

In the lower right (Quadrant 3), we find external and spiritual motivations that are often employed by people to get others to behave the way they want. Guilt, shame, and fear are pressed upon others from the outside to compel them to behave in certain ways.

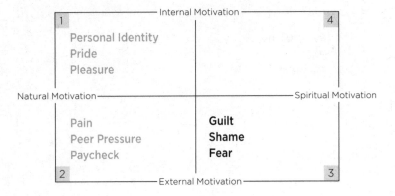

Quadrant 4 in the upper right of the diagram is the unique place of a person's heart where internal and spiritual motivations are birthed. It is a longing from inside that is available to all but must be allowed to drive us. The motivations found here are strictly optional and must be chosen and fed to become a driving motivation. These are, in a real sense, the most valuable parts of the human heart. It is in this realm where we find a passion for truth, compassion for others, and a reverence for God. The best parts of humanity are birthed within this quadrant.

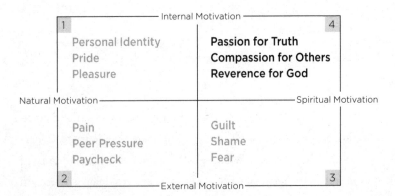

The human heart can be a very confusing place. Motives can be especially challenging to discern and understand when talking about our own hearts. Motives, however, can be impossible to understand when talking about the hearts of others. Every person is a mix of all four quadrants at once, and some motives appear to cross from one quadrant to another. However, as we look at the diagram above, we gain some clarity and are better able to see the distinctions of what gets us moving. It provides an opportunity to delineate the source of the drives we all feel.

As you look over the quadrants, ask yourself where your church's activities most often aim to move people. You may also want to ask which quadrant most fuels your actions. As a leader, you may want to ask which quadrant is the carrot or stick you most often employ to get people to act.

Each quadrant of motivation creates particular results (see the following page). External-spiritual motivations (Quadrant 3) will always result in emotional bondage, whether it is inflicted by a dysfunctional parent corralling a child or a discouraged pastor wanting to beat up a congregation with legalistic behavior modification. External-natural motivations (Quadrant 2) will always result in a form of social enslavement. Don't get me wrong; it isn't evil to be paid by your employer, but understand that the employer has a level of control over you with the money you are paid. In one sense, he or she owns you for the eight hours you are on the job. Natural-internal motivations (Quadrant 1) fuel personal drive. Only internal-spiritual motivations (Quadrant 4) can result in a sincere and selfless love. If love is our desired result, the one thing that is most important, it will come from Quadrant 4. Love is never the result of fear, because "perfect love casts out fear" (1 John 4:18). Love cannot be gained through guilt or shame either. You cannot buy love with a paycheck. Personal drive doesn't even result in love, because even when sanctified and released outwardly, it is still from a place of human nature. Love goes beyond our normal life. It is part of the image of God, but it must be redeemed. "We love, because He first loved us" (1 John 4:19). This can only come in the fourth quadrant of internal and spiritual motivations.

Motivation is an incredibly important part of the Christ follower's life. In his letter to Timothy about passing on influence to other disciples, Paul addressed the things that make up a follower of Christ who is spiritual rather than in the flesh. This theme begins in the epistle's core chapter: "Be strong in the grace that is in Christ Jesus" (2 Tim. 2:1). This is the very theme that Galatians aspires to, but the churches of Galatia were stronger in works than in grace. Paul used an interesting twist of words here: "strong in . . . grace." How does one do that? Grace is God's strength, where your own is surrendered. By definition, grace is our weakness and his strength. So in order to be strong in grace, one would have to be strong in one's own weakness. That is precisely the message Paul wanted to get across to the Galatians: they are not to work so hard to be so good. Grace meets us at the point of our acceptance of our weakness.

Paul gave the big picture of fourth-generation multiplication of disciples who are "strong in . . . grace" (2 Tim. 2:1–2). He then dove into the muddy waters of human motivation (2 Tim. 2:3–13). This passage has appeared to many to be a string of unrelated metaphors, each with its own lesson, like a list of spiritual bullet points. It is, in fact, a treatise on the motivations of a godly follower of Christ. Followers of Christ are to be motivated from within to surrender their whole lives to Christ. Why would you want to multiply anything else? Nevertheless, we often do just that. We are constantly appealing to less than internal motivations to cause the church to grow. But all those efforts in the end are in vain.

In keeping with the chart above, Paul listed three internal-natural motivations and three internal-spiritual motivations. In this critical passage about the hearts of disciples who are strong in grace and pass their influence on to the next generation, Paul devoted all his attention above the horizontal line of our chart. He left no room for external motivation. We should follow in his example. Try as we have over the years, making people behave godly without their own desire to do so is an exercise in futility at best and results in do-it-yourself spirituality at worst.

The motivation for following Christ must be internal, not external. If your faith is dependent upon inspiration, instruction, or income from an external source, you will not be able to pass anything along to others. You can invite others to come to the same place, but that will only draw more people to a single source, which would hit the brakes on multiplication to multiple generations. Everyone will need to stay close to the source of such external motivation. A vital movement of the gospel that spreads from one life to another would be the casualty of such motivating factors. And it has been.

"A worker's appetite works for him, for his hunger urges him on" (Prov. 16:26). I don't usually have to motivate myself to eat. Hunger does that for me. Most of us do not need external motivation to eat, though we likely need it *not* to eat. The food industry thrives because we all have an inherent drive to eat. Another industry that does well but exists to motivate us to not eat is the diet industry. You would think the two would be in competition, but in reality the diet business does best when the food industry does well. Ultimately, the food industry taps our internal motivation and is far more successful than the diet industry, which utilizes external motivations.

Paul appealed to the internal motivations that would keep Timothy going even in the face of hardship and setbacks. He used several analogies and admonitions to demonstrate the drive we need to have that will see us through, even in the face of suffering hardship. He begins with natural-internal motivations. The thing about natural motivations that we must understand as Christians is that we cannot be rid of them; they are a part of being human. Rather than pretend they are gone, Paul showed us that we need to surrender them to Christ so they can become sanctified.

Natural Motivations

1. A DESIRE TO BRING PRIDE TO THOSE TO WHOM YOU ARE
   RESPONSIBLE. Paul wrote, "No soldier in active service
   entangles himself in the affairs of everyday life, so that he
   may please the one who enlisted him as a soldier" (2 Tim.
   2:4).

2. A DESIRE TO BE THE BEST WE CAN BE. Paul described this motivation: "If anyone competes as an athlete, he does not win the prize unless he competes according to the rules" (2:5; 4:6–8).

3. A DESIRE TO BENEFIT FROM THE RESULTS OF OUR EFFORTS. Paul said, "The hard-working farmer ought to be the first to receive his share of the crops" (2:6).

These natural and internal motivations are not evil or wrong; they are part of our makeup as humans. When we try to lose them, we end up just pretending they are gone and slide a self-righteous mask over them—but they remain. It is far better to acknowledge them as human and surrender them to our king. That is Paul's intent in this passage, to show us that these motives can be sanctified and used for the kingdom, and that is far better than pretending they do not exist. John Piper referred to this quadrant as Christian hedonism,[2] namely, serving Jesus because it benefits us to do so. We gain a reward for following Christ, and that is not a bad thing. We have been designed by God to desire joy, and we bring him glory when we pursue it. But it is not enough in and of itself. We need more than this.

This quadrant is only the beginning of the motivation for a gospel-fueled life. These natural motivations can be useful for the kingdom, but they are not enough to truly transform the world. If these are all we have as motives, we are no different from billions of others on the planet. And we are supposed to be different. There should be something about us that the world cannot understand; we should reveal a part of God himself to the world. So Paul went on to address internal-spiritual motivations.

Spiritual Motivations

1. MOVED BY THE LOVE OF CHRIST DEMONSTRATED IN HIS SACRIFICE FOR OUR SINS. Paul charged, "Remember Jesus Christ, risen from the dead, descendant of David, according to my gospel, for which I suffer hardship even to imprisonment as a criminal; but the word of God is not imprisoned" (2 Tim. 2:8–9).

2. A COMPASSION FOR LOST AND DYING SOULS. Paul described his own motivation: "For this reason I endure all things for the sake of those who are chosen, so that they also may obtain the salvation which is in Christ Jesus and with it eternal glory" (2:10).

3. INSPIRATION ROOTED IN THE CHARACTER OF GOD. Paul reminds us, in poetic fashion, of God's faithful character. He says, "It is a trustworthy statement: For if we died with Him, we will also live with Him; if we endure, we will also reign with Him; if we deny Him, He also will deny us; if we are faithless, He remains faithful, for He cannot deny Himself" (2:11–13).[3]

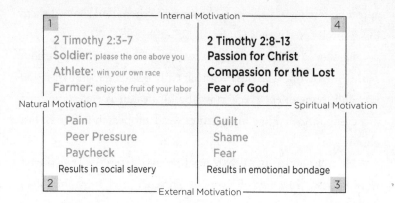

These motivations are not natural; they are, indeed, *super-natural*. When the world encounters someone moved by these things, they encounter someone they cannot understand—or stop.

This is where the Christian life is meant to be lived—in the fourth quadrant. This is where love comes from. Most of what the world thinks is love is really a selfish and/or insecure desire for personal fulfillment. This is why it seems so easy for people to fall in and out of love. Occasionally, true love is seen, a reflected image of God found in his created people. It was from this place that Jesus saved the world.

PAUL: AN EXAMPLE OF INTERNAL SPIRITUAL MOTIVATION

Paul, writing from a dark and damp hole in a rock with bars over the entrance, wrote to Timothy about the keys to a heart that would die for another. This is something he knew intimately. In one of his letters to the Corinthians, he shared with us what I consider his résumé. Those in Corinth had been led astray from believing in his apostolic gifting or calling. So he wrote to them and showed them his apostolic credentials (2 Cor. 11:23–29).

He started with a strange statement: "beaten times without number." Anyone who has ever been truly beaten remembers it and probably remembers every blow. Being beaten is not something one easily forgets. How many times was Paul beaten before he lost count?

He went on to say, "Five times I received from the Jews thirty-nine lashes." The Old Testament prevents applying more than forty lashes because it is then a lethal beating. The Jews, never wanting to violate the Law, even by accidental miscounting, made it thirty-nine lashes, not thirty-eight or forty. Thirty-eight would be too few and forty too many. This lashing was supposed to bring a man to the very edge of death. The whip used in such an instance became known as a cat-o'-nine-tails, because it was made up of several whips with lead weights attached to the ends. The whips would be woven together at the handle. Often pieces of bone were laced into some of the tails to tear away flesh when the whip was withdrawn from the victim's body. This scourging with a cat-o'-nine-tails, similar to what is shown so graphically in Mel Gibson's film *The Passion of the Christ*, was horrific. Paul went through it not once, not twice, not three times or four, but five times! His back must have been one giant scar. I have to wonder if after three such lashings he ever questioned whether he was doing the right thing. But he went on to receive the same lashing two more times!

"Three times," he said, "I was beaten with rods." The same back that had already received 195 lashes with a cat-o'-nine-tails also received a caning—not once, not twice, but three times!

He said, "Three times I was shipwrecked, a night and a day I spent in the deep." I have not met many people who have ever been shipwrecked, let alone three times. If Paul gets on your cruise ship, you'd best get off as fast as you can, because that boat is probably going down. I am just grateful Paul was not around during the time of air travel!

Paul said, "Once I was stoned." This statement alone is incredible! It is not a comment on his days in the drug culture of the sixties. There are not too many people in history who could report that they had been executed. But Paul could. When we get to heaven, we will not find very many people, perhaps only one, who can say they were executed twice! Paul was stoned in Lystra (Acts 14:19–20) and left for dead under a pile of rocks. Then his life came back, his lungs filled with air, and he rose from the pile, brushed off the dust, and walked right back into town to preach to the people! What sort of motivation is this? Where does it come from? How can someone like this be stopped?

You can threaten him, beat him to within an inch of death, you can drop him in the middle of the Aegean Sea and leave him there—and he just keeps coming back. You can't even stop him by killing him! This motivation is unstoppable! It is remarkable! It is beautiful! This is where the gospel takes root and turns someone into an agent of change who will turn the world upside down. This is the quadrant where true revolutionaries are born.

INTERNAL VERSUS EXTERNAL MOTIVATIONS

The motivations below the horizon of the diagram are common in do-it-yourself Christianity. Many churches devote much of their time, energy, and resources to working below the horizontal axis. Some throw guilt, shame, and fear at people to hold them ransom to behavior that is fitting for the church. Many rile the people up at the end of the sermon with inspiring stories spoken with gentle tones of reverence, complete with soft, stringed instruments in the background. We are so accustomed to these types of motivations in our Christianity that they are a cliché and late-night fodder for comedians.

I think the external motivation we are most guilty of employing in the church today is perhaps the external-natural quadrant. We pay people to do the needed work. In the Western church we tend to invest our money in our deficiencies, and the result is that we yield more deficiencies. When we need youth supervision, we hire a youth pastor. If we need better music, we hire musicians. If we want our kids cared for, we hire children's workers. We use money to make sure that the work is done and done well. Why? Because external motivation works. You get what you pay for. Right?

Imagine you started a McDonald's franchise because there were only a few restaurants in your town. Would you hire workers or issue a call for volunteers? Of course you would hire workers, because who would want to contribute their time and energy to flipping burgers for the cause of over 200 billion served? External motivation works, and it is not always wrong. In some contexts, it is the right motivator.

Both internal and external motivations work. But the church is not a business. It is meant to be a movement of changed lives. If we resort to paying people to serve, we have started down a path that cannot result in transformation or launch a movement of change. When we rely on external motivations to accomplish spiritual work, we end up with a counterfeit Christianity. This is what Paul said in Galatians about being motivated by external means, reducing the true gospel to a false counterfeit:

I am amazed that you are so quickly deserting Him who called you by the grace of Christ, for a different gospel; which is really not another; only there are some who are disturbing you and want to distort the gospel of Christ. . . .

For am I now seeking the favor of men, or of God? Or am I striving to please men? If I were still trying to please men, I would not be a bond-servant of Christ. (1:6–7, 10)

All the motivations below the midline of our chart result only in manipulation of some kind. Human efforts to control the outcome of other people's actions will not spread a grassroots movement. Even if it could, it would all be lost, because only what is done in love will last, and love is only truly found in the fourth quadrant.

There is something so powerful that nothing on the planet can stop it. Unleashed, the motivations found in the upper-right quadrant, when ignited by the true gospel, can turn the world upside down. These motivations not only initiate a movement, but once the momentum is released, it cannot be stopped. These motives can actually rise within people to such an extent that death itself cannot stop them. Wherever the church has faced its greatest persecution, these motives have won the day.

In the fourth century, Ambrose, a bishop of Milan, said, "The blood of the saints is the seed of the church." This is very true. Satan can do little to stop people motivated like this, except to tempt them to settle for the lesser motivations of the other three quadrants. I suspect that is a key reason why the church in the West is so stagnant and lifeless; we are not living in the upper-right quadrant.

Life itself is full of all four quadrants at work in our hearts. It is not wrong to be motivated by natural-external motivations; in fact, just being human means you have these at play in your life. The same is true with the external-natural motives of quadrant 2. Life is most often found in these quadrants, but world-changing gospel movements motivated by the love of the new covenant are not. The point of this chapter is not that you should avoid all the other types of motivations in your life. Rather, the point is that we can only accomplish true spirituality from the fourth quadrant. When we appeal to the other quadrants to get what is only possible in the fourth quadrant, we start to build a counterfeit spirituality.

An important thing to understand is that you cannot get fourth-quadrant results by applying the motivations of the other quadrants. We are deceived into thinking that if we apply pressure from the outside, people will start to love the unlovable. This never works; it only results in people feeling guilty for not loving, and this is a big difference. Love, real love, is never motivated by guilt, shame, or fear. So whenever we appeal to guilt, shame, fear, or financial reward, we are sacrificing the power of genuine love released by the gospel. We must begin to realize how much we have lost and that continuing down this path will only make things worse.

It is my belief that we often react to something evil with externally applied moral enforcement, and as a result, we actually lose the battle we are fighting—but we lose so much more than that. A reaction to sin, rather than a revolution of love, is destroying our reputation and producing a less than righteous spirituality in the church.

When we lay out seven to ten behaviors that people cannot participate in after they sign the covenant on the dotted line, we are actually making spiritual choices for these people. Their decision becomes conforming to our standards rather than following Christ.

I understand that they chose to sign the covenant. Choosing to sign a piece of paper, however, is an entirely different moral choice than choosing not to violate your conscience and compromise your faith when presented with very real temptations. Choosing to live up to our standard to keep your word to others, rather than listening to Christ and following him, is indeed a sad substitute. Even though you chose to sign the covenant, someone else made the decision of what to include and exclude from that list. It is often just as revealing what is left off such lists as what is included.

When I went to seminary, I was presented with a covenant that said, among other things, I would not dance, drink alcohol, attend movies, or play cards. Our priorities are skewed when we make such lists. If I were to follow the letter of the covenant, I could shoot heroin but not drink a glass of wine. I couldn't play Hearts, but murder wasn't on the list. And be careful about premarital sex; it might lead to dancing.

Of course, those who enforce such lists would say that heroin and homicide are, in fact, obvious sins to avoid and do not need to be spelled out, because the Bible already speaks to those behaviors. That reasoning, however, is also quite revealing. It is saying that these are laws about sins *not* mentioned in the Bible. Are we saying that the Bible is insufficient for our sanctification as believers? If the Bible doesn't condemn something, but you condemn it with the same authoritative gusto of Scripture, then you have crossed a line. Now, you are the one determining what is sin and what is not. And when you start enforcing your own rules under the authority of a signed covenant, you have become a Pharisee in every respect. When we compose such lists even with benevolent intentions, we have not helped people but rather hurt them. The Pharisees likely meant well—much of the time.

Another problem with this approach is that it begs for viola-
tion. It incites within us a squirmy response that seeks loopholes.
The other alternative is to list everything people can or cannot do,
but that would be an infinitely long list. Paul wrote that if we want
to live under the rule of law, then we must obey all of the laws (Gal.
5:3). James told us that to violate any one law is to violate them all
(James 2:10). So when we take an approach of listing rules that
must be obeyed in order to comply with our standard of righteous
behavior, we are taking on a humongous task and divine responsibility. We should never cross this line, no matter how good the idea
seems. We must learn to let people choose to follow Christ without
our getting in the way.

In an attempt to make healthy and godly decisions for people,
this method actually does the opposite—it induces sin rather than
preventing it. If I were to go see a G-rated Disney movie with my
daughters while under such a contract with my seminary, I would
be violating my word. I would be an untrustworthy liar who lacks
integrity, which is a whole lot worse than enjoying a movie. Where
there would have been no sin, suddenly there is sin for something
that should be a joyful and loving venture. That's what the law does;
it entices us to sin. What is the first thing you want to do when you
see a sign that says Do Not Touch—Wet Paint? You touch it to see
if it is true or not. That is what the law compels us to do.

While in seminary I did not choose to do any of those things,
but the covenant only kept me from a glass of wine and a good
movie that I would eventually see later anyway! It was my love for
Jesus that kept my conscience clear and my path straight, and that
is always the case. I am grateful that the seminary relaxed a bit
and changed the covenant to an easier list to live by. My daughters
could then see *The Little Mermaid* with their dad.

By far, what I think is the worst consequence of making moral choices for others is that it robs them of the one thing that is most important—love. We all need to make our own decisions, moved by the love of Jesus, rather than legislate such morality on their behalf.

I believe we often react to things with moral legislature meant to mold people into godliness, but that is not possible. We have attempted to exert righteousness from the outside-in rather than from the inside-out. This form of behavior modification does not produce spiritual people, only moral people at best.

LOVE IS A CHOICE

Christian parents often attempt to baby-proof the world for their teenagers the way they did their home when their children were toddlers. They do so by attempting to remove all bad options. We leave them only good choices, such as this Christian school or that one, hidden from the evils of the world. But this does not work; we usually end up enticing them to see what they are missing and even start to long for it. Love cannot be chosen for another. Even our compliant kids grow up to be moral but unloving, because you cannot know love unless you choose love. Love is always a choice, a choice that requires good options and bad.

Try telling your spouse, "I love you because I made a vow in front of witnesses and now I'm under contract—so I have to." See if that gets you points. It doesn't, because love is a choice. Your spouse wants to be chosen every day, not just once twelve years ago in front of a pastor, your family, and friends. Your spouse wants you to choose him or her over your smartphone, over your favorite television show, and over your favorite hobby or NFL team. When you choose them over something they know you enjoy, it means you love them more. Love begets love, and they will likely want you to enjoy those things even more. But it all begins with a choice.

The problem with allowing choices is that we run the risk of our children choosing poorly. Yes, that is a risk, but one we must take. God wants us to love him and choose him, so he does not take all the bad choices out of our way.

Jesus prayed, "I do not ask You to take them out of the world, but to keep them from the evil one" (John 17:15). That has been my prayer for my kids daily for decades. It is hard because it means you are not in control and your kids are not always safe, but it also means that they can discover love, real love.

There is a reason why God left the tree of forbidden fruit in the middle of the garden. When you think about it, the Garden of Eden was not babyproofed. There was a toxic fruit tree right in the middle of the garden, with no fences or locks to keep the man and the woman away. God's desire was not robotic people who only do what is right, but loving people. Loving people require that they have a choice of good or bad. Every day Adam and Eve had to choose not to eat the fruit and to love their Creator by obeying his command.

Unfortunately, when you allow for choices, children can make poor ones. But if we do not allow for such choice, we forfeit love, and we end up sacrificing the important reason for our existence in the process.

God wants to be your top choice. We must allow our children to choose God or they will never be real Christ followers. To make such a decision, they need to have choices—and not just positive

Christian choices. They may choose poorly. In fact, it is likely they will. But that is the path that leads to becoming loving people. God had to allow Adam and Eve to choose poorly, which cost him dearly, but he was willing to take that risk and pay that price. Can we do so as well?

When we react to sin abuses in the world with moral legislature, we abandon our true calling, we forfeit our true power, and we lose the battle we hoped to win. This reaction can only end in failure, powerlessness, and hypocrisy. Welcome to the twenty-first–century Western church. The church needs to respond to issues in ways that empower and release love rather than take a stand against people and issues and attempt to enforce morality without love.

A BETTER COVENANT

When we have people sign a covenant that restricts their choices and behavior to be more in line with corporate moral standards as a means of identifying with an organization, we are enforcing the wrong covenant. There are many covenants in the Bible. Some are unconditional and incapable of being revoked, and others are now void because of past violations. But there is one covenant that rises above all others. It is called the new covenant. At first the new covenant was an idyllic promise that was held out by the prophets of the old covenant, speaking of what would one day come. Jeremiah wrote of it and described it this way:

> "Behold, days are coming," declares the LORD, "when I will make a new covenant with the house of Israel and with the house of Judah, not like the covenant which I made with their

fathers in the day I took them by the hand to bring them out of the land of Egypt, My covenant which they broke, although I was a husband to them," declares the LORD. "But this is the covenant which I will make with the house of Israel after those days," declares the LORD, "I will put My law within them and on their heart I will write it; and I will be their God, and they shall be My people. They will not teach again, each man his neighbor and each man his brother, saying, 'Know the LORD,' for they will all know Me, from the least of them to the greatest of them," declares the LORD, "for I will forgive their iniquity, and their sin I will remember no more." (Jer. 31:31–34)

Jesus was the sacrifice that made the new covenant a reality for those who choose to accept it. His blood poured out was the sign of the new covenant and the payment for it to be ratified (Luke 22:20). When we enter into the new covenant, we are changed from the inside out. Old covenants are laws written down, which we are forced to submit to, but the new covenant is written on our hearts. Our hearts are changed, not the laws.

Paul wrote to the Corinthians about the new covenant:

You are a letter of Christ, cared for by us, written not with ink but with the Spirit of the living God, not on tablets of stone but on tablets of human hearts. (2 Cor. 3:3)

This is true spirituality. It is a new covenant that cannot be violated; your forgiveness is permanent and never in question. Under the new covenant you are shown real love, and that causes us to love in return. We love because he first loved us (1 John 4:19). We do not live a certain way under fear but rather moved by love. There is no fear in love, because perfect love casts out fear of punishment. Because all our debts are paid, all we have left is love for our Savior. We are free to choose love, and how can we do otherwise when we realize all that was given to us.

The real question is this: Why would we want another kind of covenant when we have already been given the new covenant? Why would anyone want to go back to the old covenant? To this idea, Paul said to the Galatians, who were going back to the law, "You foolish Galatians, who has bewitched you?" (3:1).

Why would we empower a man-made list of behaviors over real love that chooses Christ over all other options, no matter what temptations imagination can conceive?

To choose moral conformity to rules over a spiritual life moved by internal love as a result of the new covenant is to choose "a different gospel; which is really not another" (Gal. 1:6–7). *Gospel* means "good news." The new covenant is the best news ever to be received; it is the gospel. We are justified and made holy by the acceptance of the new covenant. Why then would you reject that covenant for an old one that never worked in the first place? That truly is foolish.

The New Testament tells a different story about a more subversive revolution that changed society for the long haul. Our typical reaction to trends and issues does not change anything other than, at best, a few laws. The love birthed by the gospel changes hearts, which can change the world and the future.

A form of godliness based on moral behavior void of love is not what Jesus died for. Truly spiritual people will make moral choices, but moral people are not necessarily spiritual. Love is the fulfillment of all righteousness and every law of God. We cannot fulfill the law any other way. The new covenant is our only hope and our only means of becoming righteous.

Conformity to rules never produces true righteousness. It produces weak people, and weak people do not change the world. We cannot change ourselves this way, so what makes us think we can change the world this way?

In much of the church today this weakness is visible among leaders who are afraid of sin and death as though Jesus didn't accomplish anything. We set up fences to try to avoid sin, and as such, we actually put more confidence in the darkness than we do in the light.

It is quite common today for church policies not to allow for a pastor to counsel a person of the opposite gender. In fact, in many churches a policy is put in place that forbids a pastor from being alone in the same room or car as someone of the opposite sex for fear that sin will result.

Really? Are Christians so weak that being alone for sixty minutes with a person of the opposite sex is enough for a pastor to abandon all faith in Christ and a holy calling for a few minutes of pleasure? Are men really that appealing to Christian women that they would abandon their love of Jesus for a brief lust connection? Do we really think that followers of Christ are that weak? If your pastors are that weak, they should not be leaders in the church at all.

In many of the churches where this kind of rule is in place, we usually find another rule as well—women are not allowed to be pastors. If a woman cannot be in a room with a pastor and there cannot be any women pastors, are we actually telling half the population of the world they cannot have a pastor simply because they are female? How ridiculous these types of man-made rules are when employed. They sound so honorable at first, but upon reflection they most always create a convoluted mess.

Do we react to the weaknesses of a few in order to determine how all the church should respond to one another in a defensive manner? Yes, I think we do. We live by a weak defensive spiritual posture that actually empowers sin and weakens Christians. We have more faith in the temptation of sin than we do in the power of the gospel or the indwelling presence of the Holy Spirit. As a result, we institutionalize (and glorify) the power of sin rather than the power of the gospel—and we do this all the time.

If we cannot maintain our sanctification while meeting with another Christian of the opposite sex for a few minutes, then what did Jesus accomplish when he died on the cross? Perhaps we are that weak because we have put our faith in do-it-yourself spirituality more than in Christ.

Someone may point out that wisdom means avoiding places where a temptress may seduce you (Prov. 5:1–23). I think that wisdom would avoid someone trying to seduce you, just as Joseph did with Potiphar's wife. However, it would be wrong (times ten) to assume every woman in your church is an adulteress looking for an opportunity to pounce on your pastor! If a truly spiritual man finds himself in a dangerous situation and feels tempted, he should flee as Joseph did. But making a blanket rule that a man cannot ever be in a place alone with a woman who is not his wife is not only putting more faith in sin than in Christ, it is also a foolish way to gain character. Real character can face temptation and pass the test. In fact, one can't truly develop deep character without the test temptation brings.

What if the woman is attractive to you? What if she is looking for support and finds you attractive? What if you are feeling lonely in that moment? What if no one else is around? I suggest you be godly because you love Jesus! Jesus is always around. If you find that is not enough, you have a bigger problem than temptation. I am not bashing all forms of accountability, but I am suggesting that setting rules like this is a foolish attempt to keep sin at bay. Rules like this are a defensive posture that is motivated by a fear of sin, not a fear of God. Trust me, if the pastor fears God, he won't mess around with temptation. If he doesn't fear God, this silly rule will not keep him from sin.

It is time for us to have truly spiritual leaders who stand against the world, the flesh, and the devil. We need men and women who put no confidence in the flesh and its silly rules. We must be a people who will storm the gates of hell with bold and reckless abandon because we have faith in Jesus more than man-made rules. We should not let a woman alone in a car stop us. Get tougher, dudes! This is an eternal battle for the souls of people, so don't be so weak spiritually, and don't empower the flesh so much.

This form of spiritual boundary-setting is actually a modernized version of blanketing women with a burka because they are too tempting for godly men to have to deal with. If we truly want to make a difference in this world, we need a tougher spirituality than this.

Avoiding temptation is smart when you can do it, but that is not always the right thing to do. In fact, if we always avoided all temptation, we would stunt our spiritual growth. Jesus did not always avoid temptation. We must be disciples who can face temptation and pass the test. If someone can rise to leadership who has never been tested, we have a problem with the way we view leadership.

The law of the old covenant is incapable of saving us. Jesus is fully capable, and the new covenant is stronger than the old. Light is always more powerful than darkness. In fact, darkness is the absence of light. I truly believe that grace is more powerful than the law, and I have been willing to bet my life on it. Granted, people will fall into sin if we allow for it, but it is not as though they will be stronger than sin living under the law.

I suggest our real problem is that we have put more faith in the law of the old covenant than in the powerful grace of the new covenant. Why should anyone want our gospel if we don't even want it? We have abandoned the true gospel for another.

The symbol Jesus gave us for the new covenant is what we typically call communion. As he took the cup of wine and passed it to the disciples, he said, "This cup is the new covenant in My blood; do this, as often as you drink it, in remembrance of Me" (1 Cor. 11:25). In the minds of the Jews, life is in the blood. The shedding of blood is the shedding of your life. When we take the cup of wine, representing Jesus' blood, we are taking into ourselves his life. That is the new covenant—the life of Jesus within us. His death brings us life, and that life flows from the inside out. That was worth the sacrifice he made for us, and it is worth living for and dying for today.

ELIMINATING THE APPEAL OF FALSE-GOSPEL MOTIVATIONS

If you are a leader who is using anything other than the gospel to motivate your people, you are part of the problem. A little of this and a little of that works great when you're making a casserole, but when it comes to the power of the gospel, it creates only poison. Some do-it-yourself spirituality mixed with some Jesus-soaked good news is not okay in any way. We cannot tolerate a false gospel and expect to produce the fruit of God's Spirit. As long as we continue to walk down the wrong path, we are taking ourselves farther away from the true destination, no matter how right the view looks. The only solution is to turn around, walk back to the right path, and start heading in the right direction. You can't mix a little poison into your pie along with all the good ingredients and expect the result to be good. Until we stop practicing the false gospel of do-it-yourself spirituality, we will never be on the right track—only further invested in the wrong direction.

Can the gospel be enough? I am convinced it is the only thing that is enough. I will live or die on that belief. If we are not willing to bet the farm on the true gospel to change lives, and instead we hedge our bets with a little do-it-yourself spirituality mixed in for the sake of practicality, then we are selling our whole selves to a false gospel. We must choose between the whole gospel or no gospel—there is no in-between.

Jesus already paid in full for your entire righteousness. Your true spirituality is already accomplished, not by any efforts on your part. Reading more of the Bible, praying more, evangelizing, or attending more church services will not gain any more spirituality than you already have been given in Christ. We cannot lose any of our spirituality or gain any more than we already have. We can, however, choose to live according to the flesh. We still have a free will, because we still have the most important command: love. What if we allow people to make a choice and they choose sin? That is what the next chapter will address.

Chapter 5

RESTORING OUR FALLEN

*If you are on the wrong road, progress means doing
an about-turn and walking back to the right road.*
— C. S. LEWIS

*Sin is not hurtful because it is forbidden, but
it is forbidden because it is hurtful.*
— BENJAMIN FRANKLIN

No one likes to be lied to or ripped off. But not knowing you've
been deceived is the worst.

There are many forms of self-deception mentioned in the New
Testament. Thinking you are more significant than you really are
is a form of delusion (Gal. 6:3). Hearing God's word but never acting on it leads to self-deception (James 1:22). Those who hold on
to their anger give the devil an opportunity to deceive and manipulate them (Eph. 4:26–27).

These forms of delusion are widespread. Perhaps the most exten-
sive delusion that has gripped not only people but infused our entire
culture is the idea that our actions have no consequences. When we

rebel against God with sin, we expect to get away with it. As long as we are not caught, we have eluded the consequences. This is a deception.

Paul wrote to the Galatians: "Do not be deceived, God is not mocked; for whatever a man sows, this he will also reap. For the one who sows to his own flesh will from the flesh reap corruption, but the one who sows to the Spirit will from the Spirit reap eternal life" (6:7–8). Even if you're not caught by others, God is not mocked or fooled.

People would prefer to believe there are no consequences for their actions. Actually, they prefer there are no negative consequences for their sinful actions. They actually want positive results for their industrious actions. But when they do what is wrong, they think they should be able to get away with it. When it is clear that someone will not get away with it, rather than attribute such justice to a holy God who sees all, they prefer to ascribe it to karma, as if the universe has an unseen balance to it, void of a personal, all-knowing God who is holy.

My dog hates when I give her a bath. It's agony for her. But she loves it when she is fresh and clean afterward. She runs around as happy as she can be, enjoying the consequences of a bath. She's a dog, so she's not really able to put together deeper concepts of cause and effect. Most people are like my dog in that they cannot make the connection between actions and consequences, but unlike my dog's after-bath-time reverie, people revel in sin and hate the consequences.

To not understand that we reap whatever we sow is to deceive ourselves. It also is mocking the holy God who is always watching. That is why a fear of God is the beginning of wisdom (Prov. 9:10).

In a book that deconstructs all the humanistic means of sin management, the natural question arises: what do we do about sin? Should we let it run rampant and not do anything about it? Since ignoring evil is never a good idea, Paul addressed sin and its awful consequences in Galatians, and I will as well in this chapter.

SIN ALWAYS HAS CONSEQUENCES

Living in a university dorm for the first time, I was thrown into a world with many very different people from a variety of walks of life all living together and sharing the same bathroom. Though it was only for a couple of years, this was a learning experience that would forever mold who I am.

When I first met Mark during that time, he informed me that he was a Christian. I was not a Christian at that time, but I was starting to seek God, so I watched Mark closely.

As the first year went on, Mark was given a name to fit his status in the dorm—Party Marky. If you ever wanted to have some chemical fun, Mark was your man. He always had some drugs available, and he was always generous with them. I avoided Mark for the most part, thinking he either wasn't a real Christian or he was somehow messed up.

During my first year in the dorm, I gave my life to Christ and never looked back. I watched as Mark continued in his lifestyle, wondering what would happen to him. During my second year in the dorm I found out.

Mark was driving his Jeep one night and something unusual happened. The windshield came loose and struck Mark's head, knocking him unconscious. His car swerved out of control and rolled. Because Mark was unconscious, his body was not tense or holding on, but flailed instead, like a rag doll. The vehicle's roll bar kept him alive, but it severed Mark's arm.

He awoke on the ground with shattered glass and blood everywhere and saw his arm a few feet away from his body. He later told
me he instantly knew what had happened, and he knew that this
was God getting his attention.

Paramedics arrived quickly and took Mark and his arm to a
hospital, where they attempted to reattach it. It didn't take. They
tried again, but again it didn't take. Finally they told Mark that he
had lost his arm. They said if they tried to attach it again, it might
poison his body and kill him. By this time, Mark had confessed to
God all his sin and devoted his life to following God. He told the
doctors to try one more time. They said it was too risky, but Mark
insisted. The third time was successful. He could move and use his
arm, though it was never quite the same, and his scars remind him
of his need to take seriously his walk with God.

After hearing that story, many may be tempted to say this is an
awful story. God would never do such a thing. Do not be deceived;
there are more important things than body parts. Jesus even spoke
of cutting your hand off if it caused you to sin, so perhaps God
would do such a thing. But the most important perspective in the
telling of this story is not yours but Mark's. He knew exactly what
God was telling him, and he heard a loving voice. So much so that
after his change of heart, Mark knew God would give him back
his arm. Mark never saw that experience as God punishing him;
he saw it as God loving him enough to show him the consequences
of his destructive life.

When Mark returned to school after a period of rehabilitation,
he was a changed man. Party Marky was DOA at the hospital. The
new Mark was again born again. He even decided to be baptized
again, because he felt this was a real conversion. He said to me,
"I know it sounds weird, but in some ways the accident was the

best thing that ever happened to me." Mark never blamed God for the accident. He never saw God as punishing him unjustly, but instead he grew closer and more intimate with his Father because of it.

A fear of God is indeed the beginning of wisdom, and there is a reason there is so little wisdom in our world. Sin is poison, and it cannot be ingested without causing damage.

Any who do ministry among the marginalized of life will know stories like Mark's. I know at least a dozen I could tell you, and in each one the person's story repeats that God was good and that the experience was one of the best things that ever happened to him or her. Don't be deceived; most of the time, we are the instruments of our own wreckage.

IS CHURCH DISCIPLINE AN EXTERNAL MOTIVATION?

Church discipline, as theologians call it, is a process of addressing someone's revealed sin by increasing awareness and accountability among church people until finally someone is excused from fellowship or repents and is reconciled. Some use the word *excommunication* for the final step of being excused from the fellowship.

Is the idea of church discipline a means of applying external motivation to someone? Are we applying external punishment to elicit correct behavior? There are only two things we get wrong in our understanding of "church discipline": one is church, and the other is discipline. In fact, I believe the term *church discipline* is a poor description of what the Bible describes. I prefer the term *spiritual restoration*. Restoration is less an exercise of punitive measures and more a pointing people toward God for hope and health. It is actually God who disciplines, not the church.

Nowhere in the Bible is the phrase "church discipline" given to the process of restoration, and for good reason. It is not the church or the pastoral staff that disciplines people in our spiritual family, but rather our Father who metes out discipline. How would your family look if your siblings gave all the spankings to one another in your father's name? If my brother tried to send me to my room without supper, I would send him to a place where he would lose his supper. Such discipline would be dysfunctional and chaotic. It is not our place to discipline others. It is not church discipline. It is, instead, the loving discipline of our spiritual Father that draws us back to him. The theological term is *church discipline*, and since I am addressing this subject, I will use that language on occasion for the sake of clarity, but understand that I believe this phrase is a misnomer that creates many abuses.

Spiritual restoration better describes the process because it is about bringing reconciliation to the people who are being disciplined by the Father. Church discipline is not our punishing someone or cutting off a cancerous part of the church body to protect the rest of us, as it is so often described. All discipline is from God and it is from love (Heb. 12:5–6). A Christian is someone who has been reconciled to God; a restored Christian is someone who has been reconciled to God too. The church is a group of restored people; the church is not the agent of restoration but the by-product of reconciliation. After all, faith is not centered on a person's relationship to the church but on one's relationship with God.

Restoration has more in common with what we call *evangelism* than our typical understanding of church discipline. In both cases, God is the one who loves, pursues, and provides forgiveness and reconciliation. In both cases, Jesus is the only hope for a fallen state. Paul describes *evangelism* as the "ministry of reconciliation," whereby we reconcile people caught in trespasses back to God (2 Cor. 5:18-21). Isn't that what we are talking about when we discuss restoring a brother or sister caught up in the bondage of sin? The word *witness* is used to describe the agent in both cases (Matt. 18:16; Acts 1:8). We are witnesses who lovingly share the truth and good news of God's love and power with those who are ensnared by the trap of sin. In a very real sense, spiritual restoration is really just evangelism of those who are falling away. In both cases, the witness is not the agent of change nor the one to whom the subject is accountable. Unfortunately, it is far from the truth that people associate church discipline with the good news even though it is exactly the same news.

In the gospel of Matthew, Jesus laid out four steps to restore one who has fallen into the dangers of sin:

STEP 1: "If your brother or sister sins, go and point out their fault, just between the two of you. If they listen to you, you have won them over" (18:15 NIV).

STEP 2: "But if they will not listen, take one or two others along, so that 'every matter may be established by the testimony of two or three witnesses'" (18:16 NIV).

STEP 3: "If they still refuse to listen, tell it to the church" (18:17 NIV).

STEP 4: "And if they refuse to listen even to the church, treat them as you would a pagan or a tax collector" (18:17 NIV).

In this chapter I want to demonstrate how we have distorted this process and turned it into a mutation. We have misunderstood both *church* and *discipline*, and the results have been devastating and cruel.

MISUNDERSTANDING *CHURCH* HAS DISTORTED THE PROCESS

I've been a pastor at a variety of churches over the years. I was on staff at what was once a megachurch. I have been a senior pastor of a suburban neighborhood church. I've also been a church planter and pastor of small home churches that were multiplying and spreading. I've also traveled around the world, training pastors of many different kinds of churches. I have a fairly broad experience of church in the world today.

We always encounter serious issues when we try to change the church into something it was never intended to be and then try to force applications from the New Testament into an artificial environment far removed from the organic context for which it was originally intended. We struggle to give prescriptions from the New Testament to a whole other species in the twenty-first century and find that it doesn't work.

I have conducted the four steps of church discipline/spiritual restoration in three types of church experiences to varying success. I will share some of my experiences below and highlight the problems and solutions I discovered over the years.

Church Organization and Hierarchy Destroys the Process

In a larger church environment I was threatened by an angry young man with a submachine gun. After many attempts to bring him to a calmer place, we eventually had to take the issue to the church. At the time I was a youth pastor, working specifically with college students, and the senior pastor and executive staff were all out of town at a retreat. I asked one of the senior elders what to do. Because he was an attorney, he filed a request for a restraining order against the young man. That may have been the right thing to do from a human point of view, but Jesus said nothing about restraining orders. Instead of announcing to the entire church that this unrepentant man had anger issues, we decided to tell only the college class about it, since they were the only people who actually knew him. And I did so on a Sunday morning.

Twenty-seven years later, this man found me. He called me and told me he was sorry, took full responsibility for what had happened, and asked me for forgiveness. He also told me that I was a good pastor back then. I was shocked and very pleased that the Father was still working in his life.

A restraining order may or may not have been the right thing to do almost thirty years ago. Certainly it makes sense when someone is threatening violence. But the goal is not to remove a brother or sister, but to restore him or her. I have found that people who are ready to use a gun and violently take a life are not really deterred because a court forbids them to be within five hundred feet of their target.

Seeing church as we did then—as a pyramid of human authority—messed up the process. I was actually in trouble with the senior leadership upon their return for having done this without their permission. I told them that being threatened with a weapon tends to bring a sense of urgency to a bad situation. I also told them that I immediately consulted the highest-ranking elder I could find. But the senior pastor was less than understanding.

When we see church as a hierarchy with a chain of command, this perspective messes up all functions, including restoration. Many churches see their leadership as anointed to make decisions for the health and management of the church, with everyone else following their lead. That, however, is not how the New Testament describes the church. I have written a good deal about this subject, so I will not go into the details here.[1] All I wish to mention here is that applying Matthew 18 in such a distorted church model is wrought with problems. Jesus did not say, "If a brother sins, go and report it to the pastors so they can fix it." All of us are to obey Jesus' commands, including Matthew 18, and until we have a church environment where that is possible, spiritual life will be managed by fallible human beings rather than led by the Spirit.

It was the actual hard line of love and the constant, unrelenting pursuit of the Hoy Spirit that eventually brought this man to change. The ranks of human authority and titles had nothing to do with this man's discipline or restoration in the end. Being shamed in front of his peers and family also did not restore him, it only inflamed the anger issue he already had. I have to wonder if his restoration could have been much faster than twenty-seven years if we had a different understanding of what church really is.

Seeing Church As an Event Dilutes the Process

As a senior pastor of a suburban community church with about 120 people in attendance each week, I ran into another restoration scenario. For some reason, choir directors and worship leaders often seem to have conflicts, and this church was no different. After repeated appointments to get the choir director to stop hating the worship leader (she would not allow him into any room where she was), I was forced to bring others into the restoration process. But she would not listen to Jesus, the Bible, me, or the church elders. Eventually we had to tell the church about it. The elders were involved throughout the process, and together we decided to write a letter to the whole congregation and then follow up with an all-church business meeting at which everyone could ask questions.

That Sunday the entire choir left the church. We canceled the cantata scheduled for the next week. Almost immediately church attendance grew to fill the loss of these people, and honestly, many of the new people are still vibrant, contributing members of that church thirty years later. It was probably the best thing we could have done for the church. Unresolved anger provides leverage for Satan to manipulate people (Eph. 4:26–27). Hatred is destructive to a soul and is also contagious. It was good for the church, but it was not actually as healthy a process as it should have been.

I learned two valuable lessons in this experience. First, after it happened, I received a call from a pastor I didn't know telling me that the same choir director had been "disciplined" from his church prior to her coming to my congregation. He also told me that she had come to his church after being disinvited from another church for unresolved anger issues. I heard that she was going to another church in town after she had left mine, so I called the pastor and told him about this pattern.

A second thing I learned helped me to understand Galatians 6:1–3 (NIV) better:

> Brothers and sisters, if someone is caught in a sin, you who live by the Spirit should restore that person gently. But watch your-selves, or you also may be tempted. Carry each other's burdens, and in this way you will fulfill the law of Christ. If anyone thinks they are something when they are not, they deceive themselves.

When I had read that passage before, I used to think, *Why would I be tempted to sin by watching the hardships and humiliations others had gone through for doing so?* Church discipline actually motivated me not to sin. During this process with the very angry choir director, these verses took on a new meaning. I distinctly remember feeling extremely angry at her for causing so much heartache for so many people. It was then that I realized that sin can be contagious in subtle ways. The Lord challenged me to forgive her. According to Paul, we are not supposed to be full of ourselves in approaching this kind of situation, thinking that we are better than the other person. Instead, we must be gentle, humble, and watchful of our own hearts in restoring a fellow believer.

When church is nothing more than an organization or a building, then church discipline/spiritual restoration becomes exclusion from attending worship services at an address. There are plenty of other churches around, and discipline/restoration from this faulty understanding of the church is futile.

How we apply Matthew 18 in this context gets murky and at times absurd. How do we "tell it to the church"? In this case, we wrote a letter and conducted a special business meeting after a church service. I've heard of some churches that print such news in their bulletin. I've seen that it has also been announced from the pulpit during the rest of the announcements. It goes something like this:

We will have a youth retreat next weekend.
There's a new overcomers anonymous group starting this
    Wednesday evening in the church basement at 7 p.m.
John Doe has committed adultery and is leaving his wife for
    another woman and will not repent, so we are no longer
    welcoming him to any of our events.

> And Jane Smith will take the morning offering, followed by
> another worship song from the band before pastor gives us
> this morning's message.

Somehow I don't think this is what Jesus had in mind when he
told the disciples to restore a church member. There are about sixty
"one another" commands in the New Testament. One of these is in
the context of church restoration from Galatians 6:2, where Paul
told us to "bear one another's burdens, and thereby fulfill the law
of Christ [which is to love one another]." We aren't able to actually
do the majority of these commands in the event that we think of
as church on Sunday mornings. But we need to understand church
from a New Testament perspective rather than the Constantinian
model inherited from Roman Catholicism.

Because church is relegated to being an audience that listens
to a sermon, which we treat as if it were a sacrament, there is so
little opportunity for the church members to share an intimate
life together. The practicing of Jesus' commands (and all the one-
anothers) is lost to us. Church discipline/spiritual restoration simply
becomes a public announcement of someone's sin to a bunch of
people who likely wouldn't know the person if he were sitting next
to them. And because they don't know the member, they couldn't
possibly obey the objective of the process. On the other hand, what
would the result be if they could obey it? Likely, the person would
no longer listen to the same sermon and sing the songs with the rest
of the congregation. He or she would only have to attend a different worship event at a different church around the corner. Is that
really what Jesus communicated? The short answer is no.

Viewing church as an event creates a climate where it's easier to
hide our dark secrets. It's a whole lot easier to hide things behind a

mask when all you have to do is greet people on Sunday mornings, and no one really delves into the grime of real life.

Having events as a church is not wrong in any way. Seeing the event as church is the problem. When being a church member is not much more than being a tithing audience member once a week, we cannot actually be the church that the New Testament describes. I believe the events should be optional, but the intimate spiritual family process should not. Even the Sunday worship service should take a back seat to our functioning as a family of brothers and sisters with our loving heavenly Father central to everything.

Church As an Intimate Spiritual Family Displays the True Process

By far the best experiences I have had trying to apply Jesus' command for spiritual restoration occurred when I was part of a new church plant that was a small spiritual family that met in a home or a business and had regular times together. We sat in a circle and looked into one another's eyes instead of looking at the back of a bunch of heads in rows. Everyone was a part of the spiritual process of the church. Everyone was open and honest. Practicing one-anothers is not only possible in this context, but it is the heart of what we do in these churches. In such a context, Jesus' words in Matthew 18 began to make sense.

I was a church planter with this brand-new church that started with people with very dark lifestyles. Every person had once been engulfed in a sinful past, and now they were becoming radical followers of Christ. Public baptisms at the beach and dramatic life change were the norm then, but that kind of mission is messy. Some fell back into old patterns, and some of those old patterns were really bad.

A young man confessed to some very troubling temptations and even a little dabbling. I brought to his attention the evil nature of what he wanted to do, but he didn't seem to care. He was infatuated with the sin, and it consumed his thoughts. I brought a friend, and we confronted him with the truth and consequences of his actions and desires. But he rebuffed us. I must say that his honesty was refreshing, but the evil was extreme and needed swift, strong action. I finally read the Matthew 18 passage to him and said that if he continued down this particular path the Father would have consequences for him, and he would lose the church family he had finally found. Prior to salvation, he was all alone, without friends or family. Upon hearing this, he immediately broke down in tears, repented, and never looked back. The thought of losing his new family meant everything to him. He is a vital part of one of the churches in our church network to this day, and he has started a few churches and is happily married.

By far this was the most immediate success I've witnessed when I've applied Jesus' command from Matthew 18. I believe it worked because the church was much more than a weekly worship concert followed by a sermon at a special building or a hierarchical organization with membership; church was a family in the truest sense of the word.

For this young man, who well remembers how lonely and close to death he was before finding Christ just a few months earlier, Matthew 18 meant a return to a life of hopelessness and loneliness. When we see church as a spiritual family on a mission together, applying Jesus' words makes much more sense. You are not publicly shaming a person from a platform to hundreds or thousands of strangers. Instead, you are informing a small, intimate family of this person's destructive path, and everyone can get involved in restoration. Often the information will not be a surprise, because people know each other so much better in this intimate setting. This does not guarantee success, but it makes a lot more sense in such a close environment.

An intimate environment is actually not a very comfortable place for someone with dark secrets. We have found that in this kind of church, confession is much more regular, and those who do not want such exposure to authenticity welcome leaving.

While this form of ecclesia makes Matthew 18 easier and more profound in its application, it doesn't guarantee favorable results. Around the same time I brought attention to God's pursuit and plan for restoration with the young man above, I also challenged a man who was taking advantage of a fragile young lady. He confessed and was apologetic initially, but he never really changed. He became obsessed with this woman, and their relationship became manipulative, immoral, and abusive. He eventually refused to stop this destructive activity. After repeated confrontations at multiple levels, I eventually told him that he had rejected Christ's leading and lordship and was bent on destruction that would hurt others as well as himself. We told the church of his lack of submission to Christ. All were saddened but not surprised. We prayed for him to change his mind, but he was obsessed with his sin and would not release it—or rather be released from it.

He left our church and went to another church in our network in another state. There he also was confronted within a short time. Because of the way church was experienced, he could no sooner get away with his manipulation there as he had tried to at our church. We all knew one another and communicated regularly. Then he went to another church and found the same response. Each spiritual family knew him and responded to him with tough love whenever he tried to manipulate others to suit his whims. Eventually he stopped trying to warp our networks and decided to stop forcing his way in. He didn't want to stop; he just agreed he was wrong and accepted everyone's challenge to reconcile or not come back. He chose to leave.

In this example, being part of a relational network of spiritual families that stretched across two states helped the church as a whole to confront this man about his issues and not let him manipulate situations to accommodate his obsessions and addictions. Eventually discipline/restoration accomplished what it was meant to do. God's Word gave this man a choice: he could continue in his destructive pattern or choose restoration.

Ten years later this man called me. He had just received word from a doctor that he had cancer and was going in for treatment. He acknowledged that he had been wrong and had caused a lot of pain for a lot of people. He confessed to the church and was immediately welcomed back. Soon word spread throughout our networks of his restoration, and all welcomed him back with open arms.

Because the woman who had been the object of his previous obsessions was part of our church, he started back in one of our new church plants, where he became a contributing part of the family. He was still quirky and had some hard edges, but the Spirit of God continued to speak to him. He became a new man. He was humbler and more responsive. He passed away a couple of years ago. He had been a thorn in my side for years, but I actually miss him now.

In this particular case, restoration eventually happened. The results of his sin, however, left lifelong scars. The next section will elaborate on why restoration in the manner Jesus described is so necessary.

MISUNDERSTANDING *DISCIPLINE* DISTORTS THE PROCESS

In my recounting these stories in this chapter, I have minimized the description of the sins involved because I don't want to elaborate on the dark pasts of some key people within our movement. I have used pseudonyms and omitted names and details on purpose. As you read these sanitized versions, you may wonder why I confronted some of these issues. Why not let people be and accept everyone for who they are?

In the above stories, the potential issues of premeditated murder, possible rape, violence, pedophilia, stalking, drug and sex addictions, child neglect, bigotry, hatred, slander, gossip, and runaway ego were involved. Most of these are not tolerated in our secular society, let alone in the church. But lest you think I was disciplining people for these sins, I want to clarify. The idea of confronting someone who is sinning is a difficult thing for many. Making these sins public is especially hard to swallow. Publicly shaming others is an awful idea and for good reason. If we think we have sufficient authority to shame people or excommunicate others, we completely misunderstand the New Testament.

For centuries the church has had the deluded idea that God has delegated its care, management, and governance to a human council while he is tending to other things. That is wrong on so many levels, but it is a functional reality in most churches today.

So church discipline/spiritual restoration has become something that we do to others. We have taken it upon ourselves to punish those who are not behaving properly. We exclude them from our organizations if they are out of line. We discipline them with the authority we believe we have been given. But I do not see that as right.

Nowhere are we told that it is our job to discipline others; that is not one of the many "one anothers" in the New Testament. We are not the sin police. People do not have to meet our expectations. We are not one another's judges. We are not the Father or the head of the church in any way.

Even in applying the commands of Christ from Matthew 18 that are about restoring a believer to fellowship, we are not the source of authority. We are simply showing people what Jesus said. When we confront people on a destructive path, we are simply showing them what the Scriptures say and allowing them the freedom to choose what they want and the consequences awaiting their own choices. It is not our authority or opinion that matters. We are simply offering people the good news of freedom from the bondage and destruction of sin. That solution, however, is not about attending a church service or being a church member. No, the only solution to sin is Jesus.

If the process is done as Jesus prescribed and Paul expounded on, people will recognize that the one they are supposed to listen to is God. In the end, they will know that God is telling them to turn around or face the consequences of the wrongs they've done. They will feel like those who are involved in the process are simply family members appealing to them for their own sake. We are a family, but it is our Father who disciplines us. We simply agree with him and acknowledge his authority.

No one will stand before you and me and give an account of their sin to us. We are not their judge and jury. We ourselves are forgiven just as much as they are. We have received mercy just as much as they have. In fact, if the restoration process is done as it is described in the New Testament, those being addressed will feel as though God is speaking to them and is fully responsible for their discipline and restoration. Personally, I do not want that responsibility, because I would muck it up. Only God can restore a person. It is his loving-kindness that leads us to repentance (Rom. 2:4). In all the above cases, wherever there was any success in restoration, it was not because of the threat of disassociation but because the subject was directed back to Christ as the only hope of salvation and reconciliation.

Our goal is to help people recognize the destructive path of their actions as they reject the authority of God in favor of bondage to sin. Ultimately, a fear of God is the aim, not public shame. The question is always a simple one: will you follow God or will you follow the dictates of sin? Acceptance into our meetings or organization should not be the ultimate concern, and when we make it such, we distort the entire process. We are just saved sinners offering another sinner the good news, which is their choice to make. As I said before, church discipline has more in common with evangelism than anything else. In fact, it is very much the same thing. Both are a presentation of the good news that there is freedom from sin and its consequences found in the person of Jesus. The evangelist does not save anyone, nor do the witnesses in church discipline.

C. S. Lewis brilliantly summarized the simple choice in his incredibly insightful book *The Great Divorce*. He wrote, "There are only two kinds of people in the end: those who say to God, 'Thy will be done,' and those to whom God says, in the end, 'Thy will be done.'"[2] The wordsmith that he was, Lewis described the gates of hell as "locked from the inside." We do not force correct decisions from people and we have no authority to demand correct behavior of others. Sin management is not our job—ever.

The fact that we so often see church discipline as a means of others' spiritual sanctification is evidence of our rampant do-it-yourself spirituality. This is clear evidence of a legalistic view of spirituality, of Galatianism. If you believe the activity of others makes you more spiritual, then you do not understand the gospel. Only Jesus can save us, sanctify us, and ultimately bring us into glory. You and I can't do any of that for ourselves, and we certainly cannot do it for others.

SIN IS A RATTLESNAKE, NOT A CREAM PUFF

Even being a passive agent of good news is at times a challenge for us. Being involved in other people's lives, especially their sinful choices, is uncomfortable and hard. I believe the reason we feel this way is more indicative of the age in which we live rather than a good understanding of the Scriptures. There is a spirit of this age that has so saturated our culture that we do not realize how affected we all are. The philosophies of the world start to sound good to us, even better than the old philosophies from an ancient book.

We think that people are generally good, and when they make a mistake, it is an aberration and not normal. Sin is a personal choice, and we should not intrude into other people's business. Who's to say what is sin anyway? What is wrong for you may be right for me. We need to progress into the twenty-first century and accept that good people do things that were formerly considered wrong but are not really so bad. There shouldn't have to be negative consequences for a person choosing to do something that used to be considered wrong in previous centuries. All of this is evidence of the delusion Paul addressed in Galatians when he wrote, "Do not be deceived, God is not mocked; for whatever a man sows, this he will also reap" (6:7). The deception Paul spoke about in Galatians is rampant in our society today.

The old evangelist Billy Sunday often quipped in his fiery sermons, "One reason sin flourishes is that it is treated like a cream puff instead of a rattlesnake." We view sin like a small weakness that is not very harmful if we give in to it. You see a fresh pastry on display and quickly the idea of savoring it crowds out all other thoughts, and so you give in. You willingly swallow the empty calories and indulge your taste buds. Sure, you will pay for it in some ways, but it tasted so good. No one will be hurt much. In fact, no one even really needs to know about this little indulgence. It only hurts you, but it also helps you to feel better. The worst-case scenario is that you might find yourself with a sweet-tooth addiction if you keep it up. But you feel like you can master it and not become a slave to it.

But that is not what sin is like. Sin is aggressive, toxic, and on the hunt. God warned Cain that sin was "crouching at the door," desiring to consume him (Gen. 4:7). "Be of sober spirit," Peter wrote, "Be on the alert. Your adversary, the devil, prowls around like a roaring lion, seeking someone to devour" (1 Peter 5:8). Sin is indeed like a coiled rattlesnake, ready to strike when you least expect it.

I grew up in a rustic part of California and have lots of experience with rattlesnakes. As a young boy, in a kind of rite of passage, I once foolishly caught a large western Pacific rattlesnake, milked its poison, killed it, and skinned it. I would never attempt such a thing now that I am older, wiser, and hopefully less cruel. You do not treat pit vipers lightly or you will be punished for it.

While hiking with a friend through a dried creek bed in the Malibu canyons, I remember talking about how the weather and topography was so favorable for rattlesnakes. My friend had a lot less experience with snakes because his formative years had been spent in Chicago. As I was talking about rattlesnakes, I stepped on one! The rattle was loud. I looked down and saw, as if in slow motion, a rattlesnake spinning around my leg with its jaws open and it fangs protruding. Instantly adrenalin shot through every cell of my body, and I took off running uphill through some wild brush. I reached a dirt fire road and was ready to go even higher. My friend, to his credit, beat me up the hill. Fortunately, the snake took off just as fast in the opposite direction. Neither of us were bit or injured in any way, but I gained an appreciation for how scary a rattlesnake looks up close.

Rattlesnakes are not to be trifled with. Neither is sin. We foolishly play around with sin, thinking it's harmless, except for a few empty calories. If we saw it the way it truly is, we would be more inclined to take it seriously.

As Paul counseled the Galatians, "Do not be deceived: God cannot be mocked. A man reaps what he sows. Whoever sows to please their flesh, from the flesh will reap destruction" (6:7–8, NIV). Sin is not harmless. It does not help you in any way at all. It is lethal, addictive, destructive, and contagious. It is not because God is up in heaven wanting to spoil all our fun and forbids sin in order to make life boring. It is because he loves us and wants to save us. As Benjamin Franklin observed, "Sin is not hurtful because it is forbidden, but it is forbidden because it is hurtful."[3]

There is a strong delusion going around that people are not that bad. With all the genocide that has occurred in the modern era, you would think people would recognize that sin is real and that people are in bondage to evil. How many holocausts must we see? How many killing fields must there be? How many genocides, how many beheadings will it take to convince the world that evil is real? How can we have so much human trafficking and still believe that people are really good in their hearts? Nevertheless, people have convinced themselves that we are actually good in our nature and getting better all the time. This is the delusion Paul spoke about in Galatians when he said, "If anyone thinks he is something when he is nothing, he deceives himself" (6:3).

I had an interesting discussion on a flight recently. The man sitting next to me had read a book that demonstrated how violence in the world is decreasing as humanity is evolving. I was in shock. I asked the man how this squares with Nazi Germany or Stalin's purge, the killing fields of Cambodia, the millions killed by Mao Zedong or the genocide in Rwanda?

He answered, "Compared with the numbers in our population today, the killings are a much smaller percentage than in previous centuries."

I then asked him, "How much violence would it take to refute the proposition? Would a billion human lives taken by other people change the postulate of the author? Would that be enough to prove his evolutionary theory wrong?"

He conceded, "Yes, of course it would."

I then mentioned that since 1970 there have been a billion human lives taken by abortions.

He rolled his eyes and said, "That doesn't count."

I said the people whose lives ended would argue that it counts, if they could. I then added, "I'm glad you made it."

Whenever mass violence is inflicted on people, those who have been denied justice are described as less than human. That was true with slaves, the indigenous peoples of North America and Australia, the Jews under the Nazi regime, and it is true of unborn humans as well. This is a delusion, and because it is deception at work, we do not even realize how bad it really is. Evil is real and rampant. Sin is also found in some of the least expected places. In fact, just about anywhere you look it is found.

My brother and I once hiked in a canyon near our childhood home. An alligator lizard, which is harmless but, as its name betrays, looks intimidating, scurried under a corrugated metal panel without my brother's notice. To mess with my brother, I casually mentioned that a rattlesnake had just slid under the panel, hoping he would lift it, see the lizard, and jump back with fear. He took the bait and lifted the metal panel, and then he slowly set it back down and said, "You're right!" I laughed mockingly and said, "That wasn't a rattlesnake. It was an alligator lizard." He said, "Oh, yeah, I saw the lizard, but there was also a rattlesnake." Now he was playing with me, but I wasn't going to let him win. I went over to prove to him it was an alligator lizard, so I cautiously lifted the panel, all the while thinking, *What if he's right?* Sure enough, a baby rattlesnake (which are the most venomous) was under the panel with the scared alligator lizard. Sin is crouching in places we never expect to find it. We do not have to go looking for it; we can find it just about anywhere. The gospel we have has relevance and need everywhere we venture in this world.

Followers of Christ should be demonstrating to the world how evil has been overcome by good. Restoration is part of that. Those for whom Christ died and rose should be walking, talking billboards of Christ's love and goodness.

CONTEXT GIVES INSIGHT INTO THE PROCESS OF DISCIPLINE/RESTORATION

So much harm is done when Scripture is removed from its context and then forced to be applied in a completely different context.

Context provides understanding and better application of truth. The context of what the Bible says about what we call church discipline sheds much light on our subject. In fact, the context actually addresses all the questions raised when delving into the subject.

We all need restoration, and every one of us needs the Father's discipline. Spiritual restoration is not simply for those who are sinning; it is for all of us who have sinned. We all need God's salvation. That's why Paul wrote to the Galatians, "If anyone is caught in any trespass, you who are spiritual, restore such a one in a spirit of gentleness; each one looking to yourself" (6:1). We all need to recognize that evil is real, and we are all participants deserving hell because of our actions. Salvation is freely given to anyone who would receive it. The delicious bait of sin is tempting to all of us, and none are exempt from its lure. We should be more understanding of those captured by it and respond with knowing grace and awareness of our own potential stupidity. In self-reflection, humility, and gentleness we approach a brother who is sinning with the good news that he can find forgiveness too. In a very real and true sense, discipline is for every one of us who call God our Father. In a very real sense then, church discipline is something we all receive all the time, and it is a normal part of the Christian life.

Just as a father shows love when he disciplines and teaches his child through correction, so God disciplines us—his children. It is the love of God that is at work in our lives that brings the discipline that changes us. "Whom the Lord loves He disciplines" (Heb. 12:6). In fact, if you are not experiencing God's discipline, you should probably be alarmed (Heb. 12:8).

You might ask, How often do you forgive someone for acting out? Well, you are not alone in asking that question. In response to Jesus' words in Matthew 18 about spiritual restoration (church discipline), Peter asked how many times he should forgive someone who sins against him. He even suggested what he thought would be the perfect number, and generous on his part—"Up to seven times?" Jesus replied, "I do not say to you, up to seven times, but up to seventy times seven" (vv. 21–22).

We should all be quick to forgive, quick to restore, and slow to exercise the fourth step of the process. In fact, I have found that if you do things right, by the time you practice the fourth step, everyone is already prepared for it, including the person who is leaving (or likely already left). We are not shaming such a person, as has been the practice for centuries in ecclesia; we are evangelizing him or her with the good news. Jesus instructed the church to "let him be to you as a Gentile and a tax collector" (Matt. 18:17). In other words, we are to view them as someone who needs the gospel. It is helpful to understand that this is written in the gospel of Matthew, by one who was a forgiven and restored tax collector.

Of course, it is erring on the forgiving side of the equation that can also create havoc. There is a fine line between keeping someone's weakness confidential and covering up a problem that is causing a lot of destruction to others. In recent decades the Roman Catholic Church is discovering this, but they are not alone. If someone is a danger to others as well as themselves, the loving thing to do is to take action.

In fact, in the same passage of Matthew 18, just before Jesus laid out the steps for restoration, he warned about causing little ones to stumble (vv. 6–9). If we find out that someone is a physical, emotional, or spiritual threat to others, I believe action is required immediately. Sometimes that action can still maintain confidentiality and be effective, but sometimes it cannot.

It is, frankly, foolishness when a forgiven sinner condemns another forgiven sinner. In fact, at the end of Matthew 18, Jesus told a parable about that very subject. He spoke of a slave who was forgiven a great debt he could never repay, and then the same slave caused all kinds of trouble for another slave who owed him only a small amount. He called the slave who was forgiven but not forgiving a "wicked slave." Do you think Jesus deliberately told that story at the same time he mentioned the steps of restoration? Of course he did, and we must pay close attention.

We are all disciplined all the time, and all of us are restored by Christ. We must see that God is always loving us and always pursuing us. He is relentless and his patience and forgiveness are always far beyond our small expectations. I am constantly being surprised with God's grace in people's lives when they blow it. I often think, *If I were God, I would have put an end to this a long time ago!* But, of course, we are all grateful that I am not God.

The whole purpose of restoration is to bring health and life back to people. Forgiveness and restoration is the reason we are able to bear one another's burdens. God desires our best, and until we realize that, we will always rebel and try to gain our best without him.

I spent a few years discipling a man who finally came to understand God's relentless pursuit and receive restoration. Gerald had been raised in a Christian home and went to church throughout his youth. He was someone who always grabbed hold of life and would try anything once. This can be an admirable quality, but it can also get you into trouble. Gerald found himself with a drug addiction and dropped out of one college and tried unsuccessfully to get into another. He became self-destructive. In fact, he even tried to kill himself by intentionally falling out of a truck in the fast lane of a busy freeway. (He didn't break a bone in his body!) But God cares about our lives even when we don't.

After being kicked out of yet another college, he bought a six-pack of beer to chase down some weed and went to the beach to do a little body surfing. The waves were big and his judgment was impaired—this is a bad combination for someone in a cycle of self-destruction. He hit his head on the sand and snapped his neck. He didn't lose consciousness, but he was unable to use his arms or legs. He was about to drown, face-down in two inches of water.

He started talking to God. He confessed his sin and reconciled himself, preparing to meet Jesus within a few moments. But God's love is relentless.

A teen trained as a junior lifeguard was on the beach, and he knew what to do. He slipped his arms under Gerald's and clasped his hands behind his head. Holding his head straight, he flipped Gerald onto his back and saved his life. Gerald could breathe again!

The kid then molded some wet sand around Gerald's head, neck, and shoulders and had someone call 911. An emergency evacuation helicopter airlifted him to a hospital, paralyzed from the neck down, but alive.

Doctors took x-rays and could see the fractured vertebrae. He was not going to walk again. Gerald had already given his life back to Jesus and would accept whatever was decided, but he wasn't yet resigned to paralysis. He had a new faith inside, a faith in Jesus the Healer and in a God who obviously and relentlessly pursued Gerald his whole life.

He asked the Father for healing, and the Father obliged. Gerald walked out of the hospital with a limp. He has always had a limp since then. Like the scars on Mark's arm, Gerald's limp is a constant reminder of God's love.

Neither Gerald nor Mark view their bodies' weaknesses as a reminder of a dark time in their past. Each step Gerald takes is a reminder of the relentless love of God. Every time Mark puts on a shirt, he is reminded of what extremes God went to in order to love and restore him. Neither of these men see restoration as a product of anything but a loving God. The scars and the limp are a sign of miraculous healing in both body and soul.

Like my dog, these men disliked the washing of discipline in the moment, but they are wildly in love with the clean and fresh consequences afterward. The results remind them constantly of both God's love and sin's poison. The author of Hebrews wrote, "All discipline for the moment seems not to be joyful, but sorrowful; yet to those who have been trained by it, afterwards it yields the peaceful fruit of righteousness" (12:11). Gerald and Mark valued the constant reminder of God's relentless love for them, and they are better men for it.

We must take the lens of deception off our eyes and see sin for what it really is—aggressive, toxic, and contagious. We must see our actions, restoration, and freedom from God's point of view rather than accept the widespread lies of our culture. Sin is not a harmless life choice that does not bear any consequences. God is not a mean, out-of-touch deity who delegates sin management to a few religious leaders. Your sin was lethal enough to cost Jesus his holy life. His life is powerful enough to give you complete freedom from the clutches of evil. Do not take any of that lightly. "It was for freedom that Christ set us free; therefore keep standing firm and do not be subject again to a yoke of slavery" (Gal. 5:1). Value your salvation enough that it becomes your one thing. In the next chapter I will describe what a one-thing spirituality looks like.

Chapter 6

THE ONE-THING SPIRITUALITY

I have but one passion: It is He, it is He alone.
—Count Nicolus Ludwig Von Zinzendorf

God can't give us peace and happiness apart
from himself because there is no such thing.
—C. S. Lewis

In the garden of Eden, God gave mankind only one prohibition: do not eat the fruit of the tree of the knowledge of good and evil. Only one prohibition, and we still couldn't keep it. Can you imagine a life with an infinite number of dos and only one don't? Undoubtedly, we would all still violate the one prohibition.

Not long after the Fall, humans started killing one another and our sinful actions demanded more prohibitions. In the first five books of the Old Testament 613 commands are given to us by Moses. But the laws do not stop there. It seems religion is never satisfied with the amount of commands and finds reasons for more. By the time of Christ the oral traditions of Judaism (called the Talmud) were used to interpret and obey the laws of Moses. It had more than 1,500 laws pertaining to the

Sabbath commandment alone. A single commandment in the Old Testament had grown to more than 1,500 laws, all dealing with only one day of the week. If you were trying to live correctly under all the commandments, it would take a lifetime just to learn them, let alone obey them.

Religion can be so complicated and exhausting. Other religions are no more helpful. Some have us continuing to try over and over again in a never-ending cycle of reincarnation, constantly pursuing perfection until we finally arrive at nirvana. How exhausting is that? Each religion demands a level of compliance and perfection according to values and codes of behavior. The number of core practices vary, but the drive to be approved does not. Buddhism has an eightfold path and Islam has five pillars.

Wouldn't it be nice to get back to the garden and have only one thing to obey? In Christ we can. The basic premise of this book is that a gospel spirituality is a one-thing spirituality. It is one thing applied to myriad circumstances, but nevertheless it is only one thing we must do. And that one thing is to love.

A lawyer once quizzed Jesus about the most important commandment in all of the Mosaic Law. Jesus replied,

> "You shall love the Lord your God with all your heart, and with all your soul, and with all your mind." This is the great and foremost commandment. The second is like it, "You shall love your neighbor as yourself." On these two commandments depend the whole Law and the Prophets. (Matt. 22:37–40)

While it appears that Jesus gave us two commandments, it really is just one. If we love God with everything, we will love our neighbor as ourselves.

In the Sermon on the Mount, Jesus gave us what is commonly called the Golden Rule, which is a synthesized expression behind the commandment to love your neighbor as yourself. He said, "In everything, therefore, treat people the same way you want them to treat you, for this is the Law and the Prophets" (Matt. 7:12). Oh, how different the world would be if we all just did that. In that one action all the law and the prophets are fulfilled.

Confronting Martha amid her hectic activity, Jesus said, "'Martha, Martha, you are worried and bothered about so many things; but only one thing is necessary, for Mary has chosen the good part, which shall not be taken away from her" (Luke 10:41–42). Jesus is telling us that there is really only one thing necessary, not 1,500, not 613, not even two. Just one.

Paul summarized the entire law in one commandment: "For the whole Law is fulfilled in one word, in the statement, 'You shall love your neighbor as yourself'" (Gal. 5:14). He explained his one-thing spirituality to the Corinthians in this way: "For I determined to know nothing among you except Jesus Christ, and Him crucified" (1 Cor. 2:2). He elaborated on this in Philippians: "Brethren, I do not regard myself as having laid hold of it yet; but one thing I do: forgetting what lies behind and reaching forward to what lies ahead, I press on toward the goal for the prize of the upward call of God in Christ Jesus" (3:13–14).

Before he summarized his one thing in Philippians, Paul expounds on everything else in a very similar manner. He said, "I count all things to be loss in view of the surpassing value of knowing Christ Jesus my Lord, for whom I have suffered the loss of all things, and count them but rubbish so that I may gain Christ" (v. 8). The word Paul used to describe everything else is the Greek word *skubala*, which is translated "dung." It is actually a slang term for excrement we are all a little too polite to translate correctly today.

Jesus is our one thing, our only thing. He is the source of our faith and our love. Love is the fulfillment of all the law and the prophets. Love is only truly possible with Jesus. "We love, because He first loved us" (1 John 4:19).

If you read the Bible, you will find that the New Testament does not establish religious holy days, a clergy system, a sacred building, or a meritorious set of practices that all must conform to in order to gain the favor of God. In fact, what the New Testament does is quite the opposite: Jesus fulfills all the Old Testament laws (Matt. 5:17) and then offers himself as payment for all of our transgressions of those same laws. In exchange for our ugly rebellion, he offers us his complete righteousness (2 Cor. 5:21). As Tony Campolo noted, "He switched the price tags."[1] In essence, we are made perfect in the eyes of God as he takes upon himself all of our sin. His goodness is transferred to our account, and all our debts and liabilities are transferred to him.

The old covenant pointed to the need and reality of a coming new covenant that would provide a true and complete salvation and transformation. The old covenant could not save. In the old religious system, people were motivated to behave better through guilt, shame, and fear. These things never saved anyone but only demonstrated our need of a savior.

All the other religious systems of the world try to conform people to a standard of behavior fitting for its own rules and worldview. The new covenant puts God's Word in our hearts so that we actually want to live the truth. The new covenant adopts us as children into God's family and gives us all the inheritance of his kingdom, without any merit on our part. We are blessed with "every spiritual blessing" (Eph. 1:3) and given everything we need for "life and godliness" (2 Peter 1:3). The very Spirit of God is placed within us as a pledge of all that is ours in Christ (Eph. 1:13–14). No longer do we do good works out of fear, guilt, or shame but because Christ has freely provided a full and complete salvation. Because we have nothing left to earn from God, we are free to love both God and others. We do not do good to merit blessings; we are fully blessed, and so we are now able to love without any selfish motivation. We have nothing to gain by our love, because we have already gained everything possible without first deserving it.

Love is the only way to fulfill the law. Obligation, duty, guilt, shame, fear, inspiration, pride, emotional appeals—none of these things are sufficient to meet the requirements of the law. Christ is our fulfillment. Christ is our faith, hope, and first love. Christ is our everything, our one thing, the only thing that matters.

PUT OFF AND PUT ON: OUT WITH THE OLD, IN WITH THE NEW

As I mentioned earlier, one of the worst side effects of DIY spirituality is that we are so accustomed to the type of goodness that is only possible by ourselves that we have no imagination for the real goodness that is possible only by God. As a result, we often see those without the Spirit of God doing better than those who supposedly have the Holy Spirit. This dumbing down of love is evident in our churches, so that few are attracted to us and are instead repelled from us.

When it comes to our true spirituality, we must recognize first that a false spirituality is of no value whatsoever. In fact, no matter how much good it claims to do, it is actually poisonous. Our God is a jealous God, and he has no tolerance for idols. His good news will not allow for any other news.

Paul said to the Galatians twice: "For in Christ Jesus neither circumcision nor uncircumcision has any value" (5:6 NIV; 6:15). If we apply that statement to the context of this book, we might as well say that neither living morally nor immorally means anything. That sounds absurd, but I assure you the quote from Galatians sounded just as absurd to the first-century church members.

Living by do-it-yourself spirituality is no better than not. All the effort we put into externally motivating righteous behavior is wasted; it is *skubala*. We see the works and want to say, "Surely some of the good it produces is of value," but according to the Scriptures it is not. So we must cease and desist. We must stop the useless and exhausting work of human-generated spirituality before we can do anything of real good.

Paul finished his thought: "The only thing that counts is faith expressing itself through love" (5:6 NIV). That's it. That's all that matters. Everything else is useless and a waste of energy and resource. True gospel spirituality is love birthed through the canal of faith that is placed fully on the promise of Jesus Christ. The promises of God must be believed to the point that we stake our actions, hope, and life on them. We must be all in for the things promised to us by God. When his promises become the ground we stand, live, and walk on, then thankfulness overwhelms our hearts. The result of this is love for God and all that he loves. This is true spirituality. This is the *one thing*. Any other form of godliness based on something else is a sham. One thing. Just one thing. You stick to that and the rest is *skubala*.

The One-Thing Spirituality

This is so important that Paul repeats himself in the very next chapter of Galatians: "Neither circumcision nor uncircumcision means anything; what counts is the new creation" (6:15 NIV). Adding to the old creation is not enough. Trying to fix the old creation is futile. We must die to ourselves and be born again as a new creation. As Paul said, "I have been crucified with Christ and I no longer live, but Christ lives in me. The life I now live in the body, I live by faith in the Son of God, who loved me and gave himself for me" (Gal. 2:20 NIV). This is the new creation. This is how faith works through love. This is the true gospel spirituality that bears fruit. Everything else is a counterfeit. Everything else is toxic.

You cannot add healthy ingredients to cyanide and expect it to be good for you. Unfortunately, that is often our approach to spirituality when we try to redeem self-righteous, do-it-yourself spirituality with the gospel and hope it will all work out better because of the addition. It doesn't purify the impure; it just taints the good stuff with false ideas.

James used the analogy of a fountain, telling us that you can't draw both fresh water and bitter water from the same spring. He added that you cannot get an olive from a fig tree and a vine cannot produce figs (James 3:11–12). We need to stop expecting real spiritual fruit from human-generated spirituality that conforms behavior by using outside pressures.

You can use external pressure to carve a human figure from a slab of marble, but while it may look lifelike, it is as dead as a stone. There will be no beating heart, no circulating blood, no lungs taking in oxygen. It's just a rock shaped like a human. A true human body is formed from the inside out with the multiplication of living cells that contain the necessary DNA to code the development

| 139 |

of life. You cannot create a human being by cutting away excess stone, and you cannot make a new creation with the old means that never worked in the first place. If it did work, as Paul said, "then Christ died needlessly" (Gal. 2:21).

To the Corinthians, Paul wrote, "Therefore, if anyone is in Christ, the new creation has come: The old has gone, the new is here!" (2 Cor. 5:17 NIV). The old way and the new way cannot be coordinated. They are not complementary but hostile to one another.

So the first step to walking in the new life is to die to the old. Only when you have killed the old man are you capable of being filled with the Spirit and letting the new man grow and thrive.

Paul often referred to taking off the old man and putting on the new. Like clothes, we must first take off the old before we can put on the new. What would happen if I decided to keep my clothes on and just put new clothes on over the old ones every day? Answer: I would get thicker and thicker and the stench would compound daily. This is foolish, but what we often call discipleship is exactly like that. So much of what is done in the Western church is putting more stuff on over the old as if more stuff will make us better. Another teaching, another small group, another podcast, another book, another service project, another mission trip. This is all you need to become even more godly. Attend this church service, go to this conference, don't miss the next seminar, take this new class, and it will make you better. It doesn't. It just makes us heavier, slows us down, and makes us stink more. It looks stupid. It costs lots of money and wastes resources as it contaminates more and more of our wardrobe. It doesn't produce a disciple who can truly change the world. If it could, it would have already. Eventually it ends up repelling the people of the world, or worse, enticing them into the same false spirituality. We must stop this circus.

The only way to really be clean and healthy is to take off the old—get naked—and put on the new. If we are unwilling to become vulnerable before God and others, we will never live out the new life. John said that if we confess our sins before others, God will forgive us and cleanse us of all unrighteousness (1 John 1:9). James said that if we confess our sins to one another, we would be healed (James 5:16). Forgiven, cleansed, and healed from within—this is the start of a true spiritual life.

It is no secret that the world sees hypocrisy when it looks at the church. Being hypocritical is when we wear the right label on the outside but are full of ugliness on the inside.

Jesus rebuked the religious leaders of his day with these striking words:

> Woe to you, teachers of the law and Pharisees, you hypocrites! You clean the outside of the cup and dish, but inside they are full of greed and self-indulgence. Blind Pharisee! First clean the inside of the cup and dish, and then the outside also will be clean.
>
> Woe to you, teachers of the law and Pharisees, you hypocrites! You are like whitewashed tombs, which look beautiful on the outside but on the inside are full of the bones of the dead and everything unclean. In the same way, on the outside you appear to people as righteous but on the inside you are full of hypocrisy and wickedness. (Matt. 23:25–28 NIV)

A true gospel spirituality is a surefire cure for hypocrisy. In fact, it is the only anecdote to that poison because it cleanses us on the inside. So the first step in true gospel spirituality is to clean out the inside and make room for the life of Jesus. For most of us there is far too much of us and no room for him.

We must put off the old before we can put on the new. This is the pattern Paul set up and reinforced in every place he ever worked. It is essential for the Christian life. It is as essential spiritually as breathing is physically.

This is part of Paul's universal pattern to produce quality disciples who could, in turn, pass on the pattern to others. My friend and mentor Thom Wolf is a biblical genius. He was the first to unlock from the New Testament the missional concepts of *oikos*[2] and *person of peace*.[3] It was Thom who first revealed this discipleship pattern to me in the New Testament, and ever since he did, it is easy for me to see it everywhere.[4] In order for multiplication to occur from one life to another, certain characteristics must be evident in the people so that a simple pattern emerges that is living, authentic, and reproductive. Paul had such a pattern and constantly referred his spiritual disciples to it.[5]

The pattern has the following four characteristics if it is to initiate a multiplication movement:[6]

1. It is *incarnational*: The pattern must be internal and work its way out into behavior. Paul challenged the Philippians to follow his example and observe others who lived by *the same pattern* (3:17, emphasis mine).
2. It is *viral*: The pattern must be contagious and simple enough to pass on to other succeeding generations. In 2 Timothy 2:2, Paul referred to this pattern when he reminded Timothy of *the things he heard from him* among "many witnesses" and was now passed on to four generations (emphasis mine).

3. It is *transformational*: Because the pattern is so life changing, others also pass it on because they have been so affected by its positive transformative nature. It is sticky, so it remains and cannot be easily forgotten. Paul mentioned to the Roman believers, even though he had not yet visited them, "Though you were slaves of sin, you became obedient from the heart to *that form of teaching* to which you were committed" (Rom. 6:17). I believe that form of teaching was Paul's universal disciple pattern.

4. It is *universal*: The pattern must work across all racial, economic, political, social, language, and cultural barriers if it is to change the world. Paul wrote to the Corinthians about the pattern and said, "Be imitators of me. For this reason I have sent to you Timothy, who is my beloved and faithful child in the Lord, and he will remind you of *my ways* which are in Christ, just *as I teach everywhere* in every church" (1 Cor. 4:16–17). Note that Paul's ways were applied in every field and taught in every church.

The pattern of a Christ follower is not just something that Paul taught. Because it is universal, we also find the same pattern in Peter's and James' writings as well. The putting off and putting on is definitely part of that pattern as seen in the following exhortations from the New Testament:

• Put aside anger, wrath, malice, slander, abusive speech, and lying. In their place, put on the new self, specifically compassion, kindness, gentleness, patience, forgiveness, love, and peace. (Col. 3:8–15)

- Put "aside the old self" and "put on the new self." (Eph. 4:22, 24)
- Put "aside the deeds of darkness and put on the armor of light. . . . Put on the Lord Jesus Christ." (Rom. 13:12–14)
- Put "aside all filthiness and all that remains of wickedness, in humility receive the word implanted, which is able to save your souls." (James 1:21)
- Put "aside all malice and all deceit and hypocrisy and envy and all slander, like newborn babies, long for the pure milk of the word, so that by it you may grow in respect to salvation." (1 Peter 2:1–2)

It seems clear that the Christian life is to involve an intentional removal of the old life in order to replace it with the new life. We cleanse the old man by confessing our sins and filling that void with the Spirit of God. It is as basic to the Christian life as repent—put off—and believe—put on (Mark 1:15; Acts 19:4). It is as essential as breathing: exhale the toxic carbon dioxide and inhale the fresh oxygen.

BE FILLED: THE SPIRIT AND WORD OF CHRIST

It is not enough to remove the old patterns of destruction; we must fill that void with what is good. In Romans, Paul exhorted, "Do not be overcome by evil, but overcome evil with good" (12:21). You cannot get rid of darkness with more darkness. The only solution to darkness is light. Darkness is the absence of light.

As we confess the sins of the old, we must be filled with the new. So the next part of the pattern that the New Testament presents to us is to be filled. In Ephesians, Paul said, "Be filled with the Spirit" (5:18). In Colossians, he said, "Let the word of Christ richly dwell within you" (3:16). In both passages he described the result of being filled as basically the same: "speaking to one another in psalms and hymns and spiritual songs" and "thankfulness in your hearts to God" (Eph. 5:19–21; Col. 3:16–17). Many have trouble reconciling the filling with the Spirit and the word of Christ dwelling within, but I believe these are the same thing. The Holy Spirit brings us the voice of our Shepherd, and that is the word of Christ dwelling richly within us.

It all comes down to hearing his voice and having the courage to obey it. This is not about simply having a good hermeneutic and building a theology around it. The Pharisees had a good theology of the Scriptures and missed everything important. Jesus said to them: "You search the Scriptures because you think that in them you have eternal life; it is these that testify about Me" (John 5:39).

We often confuse the word of Christ with Scripture. Do not think I am saying that Scripture is not God's word; I am not saying that. I am saying that God's word is not just the Scriptures. Jesus himself is called the Logos, meaning "Word" (John 1:1, 14). When we see sixty-six books bound in leather as "the only word of God," we will miss some of the most important and essential truths for the new life. We will become Pharisaical and have a Christianity *about* Christ but not *with* Christ. Our hermeneutic becomes our guide and helper rather than the Spirit of God. I am not against sound interpretation of the Scriptures, but having the helper will trump historical, grammatical hermeneutics any day. Jesus said, "But the Helper, the Holy Spirit, whom the Father will send in My name, He will teach you all things, and bring to your remembrance all that I said to you" (John 14:26). The writer of Hebrews contrasted how God spoke in the Old Testament through the prophets and the written word, but how now he speaks through Jesus: "God, after He spoke long ago to the fathers in the prophets in many portions and in many ways, in these last days has spoken to us in His Son" (1:1–2).

This inner voice of God is so essential that the movement of Christianity is actually described by Luke in the book of Acts as simply "the word" (8:4). Luke doesn't call it Christianity or the church or church planting movements; the spread of God's movement is the spread of his *word* by the Spirit.

When we read Acts, it becomes clear that the word of God fueled the growth and expansion of the church. To gain a perspective of the power of the Word in spontaneous church expansion, let's start with Luke's account of the church multiplication movement in Asia Minor. We'll take a brief walk backward through the book to track the spread of the church to that point. You will see how the word of God ignites passion and spreads new life in Christ like a wildfire until an empire is ultimately overcome.

- "So the word of the Lord was growing mightily and prevailing [in Asia Minor]" (19:20).
- "This took place for two years, so that all who lived in Asia heard the word of the Lord, both Jews and Greeks" (19:10).
- "And he [Paul] settled there [in Corinth] a year and six months, teaching the word of God among them" (18:11).
- "And the word of the Lord was being spread through the whole region [of Pisidian Antioch]" (13:49).

- "But the word of the Lord continued to grow and to be multiplied" (12:24).
- "Therefore, those who had been scattered went about preaching the word" (8:4).
- "The word of God kept on spreading; and the number of the disciples continued to increase greatly in Jerusalem, and a great many of the priests were becoming obedient to the faith" (6:7).

The early church was not as blessed as we are to have multiple volumes of Scripture in a variety of translations. But they did have the word of God and it went viral!

We are privileged to have so many translations in our phone, literally at our fingertips, at all times. But we are not seeing nearly the rapid, spontaneous spread of the gospel as those who lived in the first century. Perhaps we have substituted God's voice for a good interpretation of ancient documents. I think we are missing something when we only think of God's word as the Bible. The Scriptures are the word of God, but God's word is more than that.

The word of God can also be translated as God's *message* or his *speaking* or *voice*. This is an important distinction when we are discussing a movement of God. In the book of Acts, the Gideons were not placing Bibles on motel nightstands, but God's people were hearing his voice and spreading his message. I believe that is what Luke meant when he wrote, "The word of God spread" (Acts 6:7 NIV). There is a Greek word for what we think of as the Bible in the New Testament: *graphe*. And it is translated as "scriptures," because *graphe* means the written word of God. Luke, however, does not say that the Scriptures were spreading, but that the word of God was. We are not to be filled by the Scriptures but by the voice that wrote the Scriptures and is living now.

When we have the indwelling Spirit of Christ, then we will fall deeply in love with the written Word, because it tells us more of our God. We will hear the voice of our God in the Scriptures and it will come alive within us. We will know his voice better in moment-by-moment leading as we listen to his voice more in the Scriptures. But do not put the Scriptures above the inner voice of the Holy Spirit, or you will end up with a counterfeit religion. One cannot love the voice of the Shepherd and not value the Scriptures, but you can love the Scriptures and not value the voice of God.

Doesn't that leave us open to all kinds of misinterpretations and abuses of the Bible? Doesn't that allow people to justify all kinds of strange behavior in Christ's name? Well, no more than we are already seeing, but, yes, I suppose it does. What is our defense against abuses? According to Jesus, our defense is the very thing that leaves us vulnerable. He said, "The sheep follow him because they know his voice. A stranger they simply will not follow, but will flee from him, because they do not know the voice of strangers" (John 10:4–5). Apparently, the inner voice that we must trust is trustworthy. True followers who learn to know and follow that voice will not be led astray. There will always be false teachers, and many will lead some away, but if we don't trust the Author of the Bible and instead put our trust in the systems of human teachers, we will guarantee that our religion is a false religion. I suggest we have already sacrificed a vibrant expression of the living, indwelling presence of Christ for a teaching-centered religion made up of people who interpret ancient documents. A static, rigid, lifeless religion has been more acceptable than the living, dynamic presence flowing in and through all of his followers.

The leading of the Spirit within, the voice of Christ, is so essential to our true spirituality that the New Testament seems to indicate it is the primary evidence of a true follower. Look at the following passages:

- "My sheep hear My voice, and I know them, and they follow Me; and I give eternal life to them, and they will never perish; and no one will snatch them out of My hand" (John 10:27–28).
- "However, you are not in the flesh but in the Spirit, if indeed the Spirit of God dwells in you. But if anyone does not have the Spirit of Christ, he does not belong to Him. If Christ is in you, though the body is dead because of sin, yet the spirit is alive because of righteousness. But if the Spirit of Him who raised Jesus from the dead dwells in you, He who raised Christ Jesus from the dead will also give life to your mortal bodies through His Spirit who dwells in you" (Rom. 8:9–11).
- "As for you, the anointing which you received from Him abides in you, and you have no need for anyone to teach you; but as His anointing teaches you about all things, and is true and is not a lie, and just as it has taught you, you abide in Him" (1 John 2:27).

Once you have confessed your sin and opened your heart to the indwelling presence of the Spirit of God, it boils down to listening and obeying. Paul referred to that as "hearing with faith" (Gal. 3:2).

It all comes down to who you're listening to. Do you hear the inner voice of the Spirit or are you listening to the flesh and the law (Gal. 4:21; 5:16–18)?

ON MISSION: HOLDING GROUND
AND MOVING FORWARD

The final part of the universal pattern of a disciple is to move forward, armed with faith in Christ, against the Enemy's attacks. We do not fight against people. People are pawns. The true enemy is spiritual in nature (Eph. 6:12). Our fight, our stand, is against the forces of the spiritual domain. We are saved to bring salvation to others. As we become missional individually and as a people, we will find increasing opposition against us driven by demonic forces.

So the pattern must begin with turning down the volume on the things that bring death so that we can hear the true voice of our Shepherd leading us to life. We clean out the inside by putting aside all that once held our affection and devotion and confessing it. Then we fill that vacuum with the new life of God's indwelling Spirit. From that new life within, the rest of the way is really quite simple—not easy, but simple. Paul said,

> But I say, walk by the Spirit, and you will not carry out the desire of the flesh. For the flesh sets its desire against the Spirit, and the Spirit against the flesh; for these are in opposition to one another, so that you may not do the things that you please. But if you are led by the Spirit, you are not under the Law. (Gal. 5:16–18)

We are to hear and obey. We must have ears to hear what the Spirit is saying and feet to follow. We take the presence and power of the living voice of God with us into our mission. One cannot accept the God of the Bible and not embrace his mission.

The gospel itself has the word *go* in it. Good news is to be told to others; it wouldn't be called good news if we were not supposed to share it with others. Our own spiritual life grows as we take it to the streets and start to live it out before others.

I firmly believe that when disciples are full of the Spirit and listening to Christ's voice within, we will see the advancement of the kingdom into a broken world. When we fall deeper in love with Jesus, we will love what he loves. Jesus loves people—mean, nasty, unlovable people. The true mark of a follower of Christ is love. Love is the *one thing*. It is what moves us, or we are wasting movement. We will be identified as his followers by our love for one another (John 13:35), our love for our neighbors (Gal. 5:14), and our love for our enemies (Luke 6:27–28). I think that pretty much covers it.

There is not any way to truly love without the good news. Love is the fruit of the Spirit (Gal. 5:22–23). Love results in joy, peace, patience, kindness, goodness, faithfulness, gentleness, and self-control. There is no kind of good works that can produce that, compete with it, or win against it. We must be indwelt with this Spirit by turning from everything else but Jesus and being filled by his word. And then we walk, led by the Spirit.

I cannot help but wonder what would happen if this kind of spirituality increased and the false morality of a duty-filled, do-it-yourself spirituality decreased. I imagine we would see more persecution. I imagine we would also see far more fruitfulness.

This is what it means to live a one-thing spiritual life. This is what being Christlike really means. In the next section we will look at what Christ was really like in relation to the kinds of issues we face today.

THE HEART OF A REVOLUTIONARY

Chapter 7

JESUS TAKES ON WEALTH

*True generosity is measured not in how much
we give but in how much we have left.*
—SHANE CLAIBORNE

*If I have money in my hands, I get rid of it
quickly lest it make its way into my heart.*
—JOHN WESLEY

Since the economic crisis of 2008/2009, most have felt that
their financial footing is shakier than ever. In fact, for the vast
majority, spending power has decreased and financial confidence
has evaporated. Businesses are afraid to hire, and unemployment
is a daunting reality. Our government is quick to manipulate the
numbers to have talking points about an improving economy and
job market, but lives in the real world tell a different story. We do
not have confidence in the economy, and our finances are worse
today than they were five years ago or even ten. But this is not true
for everyone.

According to a Forbes study cited in an Oxfam report, the number of billionaires in the world has doubled since the financial crisis,

from 793 in March 2009 to 1,645 in March 2014. The report, titled "Even It Up: Time to End Extreme Inequality," noted that the 85 richest people in the world have seen their wealth increase by $688 million per day. That is an increase of $500,000 per minute.[1] That is beyond our ability to fathom. To make $30 million an hour is obscene. The only thing that is more unbelievable is to imagine spending that much money at the same pace. Impossible. So that begs the question, what is that money for? What could one person do with so much wealth? Why? At what point do you say, okay, I now have enough of the world's wealth; I do not need any more.

But while the rich get richer, the poor seem to be getting poorer. There is an obscene gap between the wealthy and the rest of the world. This inequality screams at us to make a change. We need a revolution. But is a Robin Hood revolution that steals from the rich and gives to the poor the answer? Is redistributing the wealth the fair way to go? Haven't we witnessed the failure of communism? Though I would vote in favor of certain reforms and am very bothered by the way we had to bail out multibillion-dollar corporations, I personally think if we put our confidence in *any* government or *any* party to fix the problem we will all lose—well, not really all of us. One percent seems to do all right no matter what happens.

The gap between rich and poor, the haves and have-nots, is nothing new. In fact, it is as old as mankind. We live in a fallen world, and one thing I have learned is that it isn't fair and it is never going to be fair. All I can hope for is to be fair-minded myself and to treat everyone with love and respect. In this chapter we will look at how Jesus viewed money and how he responded to those who were obscenely rich.

JESUS' VIEW OF MONEY

Much to the chagrin of people on both sides of the issue, Jesus neither welcomed nor excluded those who were rich simply because they were rich. Their bank accounts meant nothing to him. He was neither impressed nor repelled by those who were extremely rich. In a sense, rich and poor suffer from the same deception: they believe money is more important than it actually is. This seems to paralyze some, derail others, and distract all. Before we can look at Jesus' response to the rich, let's look at his view of money in general.

Even Jesus' own bank account meant nothing to him. Among his band of followers was a professionally trained accountant, Matthew. But Jesus gave his financial holdings to Judas, the only thief on the team (John 12:6). Was that by accident? Was Jesus duped, or did he have values far different than our own? He instructed us not to store up our treasures on earth—he didn't (Matt. 6:19). We would all do better if we adopted a similar perspective and did not put all our confidence in our bank accounts and tangible assets.

Jesus sent his disciples out without financial backing (Luke 9:3; 10:4) and instructed them to not make money either (Matt. 10:9)—no credit cards, no support raising, no savings. This type of experience was repeated for the twelve when Jesus first sent them out without financial support (Matt. 10:1–42), and then later with the same twelve being a part of the seventy (Luke 10:1–20). After they proved fruitful twice without money and able to go completely on faith, he then instructed the disciples to take some money with them on the next trip (Luke 22:35–36).

Twice he tells them not to take a purse, and later he tells them to take one. Is he contradicting himself? Is Jesus confused? I heard

Dallas Willard comment on Jesus' changing his command to the disciples about not taking a money purse (Luke 10:4) and then taking one (Luke 22:36): "I don't think you know how to handle a purse until you know how to go without one."[2] I suppose that once you realize how little you need money you are then better prepared to handle the money that comes to you. We should all try to pass this test.

This idea seems to get to the heart of Jesus' response to money. It appears that proving you can go on faith is an important ingredient, but money itself is not. We unfortunately usually mix these two ideas rather spectacularly.

Even when he spoke about gaining returns on investments, he seemed to expect us to have miraculous returns (Matt. 25:14–29). We can only get that kind of return with great risk—and great faith. Money is only a tool in the kingdom, and it is considered by Christ to be a small thing (Luke 16:1–13). Money is used consistently to prove us faithful or unfaithful. People are important, not money.

Money seems to be a test of our hearts and faith (Matt. 6:19–21). In fact, it's more important to Jesus how we respond to money than what actually happens with the money itself. Our hearts are way more important than our money.

After telling the parable of the unrighteous steward who used money to make friends and secure his well-being with relationships instead of a retirement fund, Jesus said:

> He who is faithful in a very little thing is faithful also in much; and he who is unrighteous in a very little thing is unrighteous also in much. Therefore if you have not been faithful in the use of unrighteous wealth, who will entrust the true riches to you?

And if you have not been faithful in the use of that which is another's, who will give you that which is your own? No servant can serve two masters; for either he will hate the one and love the other, or else he will be devoted to one and despise the other. You cannot serve God and wealth. (Luke 16:10–13)

I fear we often sacrifice true riches for what Jesus called "unrighteous wealth." I am very confident that Jesus knows what true riches are, and if we are satisfied with less, we are being fools.

Jesus seems to measure generosity based on heart felt sacrifice rather than volume (Mark 12:41–44). When it comes to trying to balance generosity and stewardship, we usually land heavily on the stewardship side of the equation, but I think we should fall deep on the generosity side. In a sense, the more generously you live, the more opportunity you have to demonstrate love and faith. In contrast, the more we bank, the less we live by faith in God's provision and the less loving we are to others. I believe that much greed and selfishness is justified with the word *stewardship*. Even the way we give often has strings attached to make sure things are done the way we would do them, and this is always excused as good stewardship.

Jesus clearly told us to not give with strings attached to steer the "investment." He said, "But when you give to the poor, do not let your left hand know what your right hand is doing" (Matt. 6:3). It is rare these days to find someone with money who has learned these lessons, even though the Gospels are quite clear on these rudimentary principles. Often, those who make money are businessmen, and they handle giving with the same business mind-set that made that money in the first place. In fact, they usually call their giving an investment, and they look for a return on their investment to justify making the investment in the first place. Their right and left hands are not only aware of one another, but they are grasping the wheel at ten and two to steer the investment.

Investing is a different idea than giving, and we should be careful not to confuse them. Investing has personal gain in mind; giving is thinking of another's gain without benefit to the giver—or even at its expense. So when wealthy people invest in a ministry, they have a connection with the results, even if it doesn't produce a fiscal benefit for them. Sometimes that benefit is nothing more than feeling good about oneself. There are many other returns on an investment. One can gain influence over the strategic use of resources in a church or ministry by investing money in it. One can gain political power in an institution this way. One can gain praise and accolades. There are many returns on investments, and this is one reason why so many keep both their left and right hands securely on how the investment works out after the money is exchanged. But this is not Jesus' way of giving.

So what if you give to something that doesn't deliver a return with loads of fruitfulness? The way Christendom behaves, I would think wasting money on low-yield investments or spending it freely on people without accountability is the worst sin one can commit with wealth. Let's see how that squares with the practices of Jesus.

We already noted that Jesus did not seem concerned that Judas pilfered from the group's purse. I find it interesting that he financially rebuked Judas, not for embezzling money, but for enviously questioning a large sum of money splurged on a luxurious item with a single use (John 12:1–8). Frankly, most churches would side with Judas on the indulgent item and strongly rebuke him regarding the embezzlement. Jesus did exactly the opposite. It appears that Judas' lack of generosity was far worse in Jesus' value system than his embezzling of funds. Isn't that curious?

Jesus was more pleased by a widow's penny than a large endowment by a wealthy investor. I doubt there are many churches that would say the same. We have seen how Jesus wants us to give without a second thought or secondary manipulation—don't let your left hand know what your right hand is doing. Our foundations, endowments, churches, and ministries, on the other hand, care very much how money is spent after it is given. Clearly, the way we see money is far removed from the way Jesus did.

Unlike Jesus, we still think money is more valuable than it really is, and that gets us into all kinds of trouble. As Paul wrote: "For the love of money is a root of all sorts of evil, and some by longing for it have wandered away from the faith and pierced themselves with many griefs" (1 Tim. 6:10). Perhaps it is the lure of mammon (wealth) that has taken us so far away from faith and from Jesus.

Shane Claiborne pointed out, "A constant thread in Scripture is that we are not to take more than we need while others have less than they need, a radical critique of the world we live in."[3]

So, according to Jesus, what is the worst thing we can do with money? Here are the sorts of things Jesus rebuked regarding money usage:

- love it
- horde it
- covet it
- withhold it
- trust in it

- use God to gain it
- not give to those who need it
- profit from the suffering of others
- use it to look spiritual in the eyes of others
- think you are better than others because you have it

Read that list again and ask yourself if any of these financial sins are common in today's church. You and I both know they are prevalent. I'm convinced that today you can do all of the above and be thought of highly by the church as long as you mask it with a reverent smile, a spiritual slogan, and regular donations. Sadly, if you give recklessly, you can be considered a poor steward with your money and wasting God's resources. If the person you give money to buys alcohol, then you have been fiscally irresponsible, but is that truly a biblical idea? No; in fact, Jesus provided the wine for the wedding party in Cana, and he indulged the party-goers with the best wine and lots of it (John 2:1–11). He also didn't police who drank and who didn't. This is, again, a curious observation in light of the church's current practices.

I am never truly responsible for the decisions of other adults; I am only responsible for my own. As Paul wrote, "But each one must examine his own work, and then he will have reason for boasting in regard to himself alone, and not in regard to another. For each one will bear his own load" (Gal. 6:4–5).

This does not excuse an individualistic spirituality that is independent and irresponsible to others, but we are culpable for our actions and others are for their actions. So I am responsible to be generous with the money in my care, to use it with the love God births in my heart, but I am not responsible for the spending of anyone to whom I give it.

Wisdom has a place in this. It is not wise to invest in someone who is always making financial mistakes, but lacking wisdom is not sinful; it is just not strategic. The concern, however, is not how you are giving your money in such cases, but rather what is the best help you can be to the one who is a fiscal mess. What is the most loving thing I can do for this person? Sometimes that answer is not to indulge a gambling habit or drug addiction. I find in most cases there are ways to help without hurting. I suggest we err on the side of generosity in all matters before we start teaching lessons. Perhaps our lessons would be heard more easily if we did.

It is interesting that Jesus nowhere told us that we can sin by giving our money away too much or giving it to people without a receipt and accounting for what is done with it later. I'm not suggesting that we be irresponsible with money—I'm suggesting that we already are. From a kingdom economy, being less than generous is indeed irresponsible and lacks faith. I do not see how you can read the New Testament and come away with any other understanding. As I said, we often justify greed and selfishness with the word *stewardship*.

JESUS ENCOUNTERS THE WEALTHY

Jesus and his disciples were making the long trek from Galilee to Jerusalem at the time of the Passover, as they had several times before. This trip, however, was different for Jesus. He knew that this would be his last. Hanging over his head was the knowledge that he would be the Lamb to be slaughtered for the redemption of all. That knowledge never left his mind but informed every encounter along the way.[4] He would bring it up several times on the path, so we know he was thinking about it.

On this journey Jesus encountered two very wealthy men. In a string of three stories, Luke showed us how Jesus responded not only to wealth but to the gap between wealthy and poor. These stories are meant by Luke to run together and teach us something that individually gets lost. Hopefully we can learn how to approach people with the grace and truth Jesus did.

We will look first at the two encounters with wealthy men: the rich young ruler (Luke 18:18–23) and Zaccheus (Luke 19:1–10). Both of these meetings occurred on Jesus' final trek up the road to Jerusalem.

Jesus and the Rich Young Ruler

Imagine if a wealthy young leader walked up to you and said, "Good teacher, what must I do to inherit eternal life?" (Luke 18:18). After you picked your jaw up off the floor, you'd probably recite the four laws, say a prayer, and sign him up for your church newcomers' class, right? That is not what Jesus did, not at all.

First, Jesus did what he often did; he answered the question with another question: "Why do you call me good?" He then said, "No one is good—except God alone" (v.19). After that he said, "You know the commandments, go and do them."

I doubt that would be the response any of us would have had. In fact, if this were on a test in my theology class at seminary, and I answered it the way Jesus did, I would fail the test. We all know you cannot get eternal life by keeping the commandments (Gal. 2:16). Haven't you been reading this book?

So then, if you cannot gain eternal life by keeping the commandments, why did Jesus point the rich young ruler to the law? Didn't Jesus know how this works?

Yes, he did, and he also knew what was going on in the rich young ruler's heart. Jesus realized that the wealthy young man struggled with something most wealthy young leaders do: pride. This is evident by the young man's response to Christ's answer: "All these I have kept since I was a boy" (v. 21). In other words, "I'm perfect as is."

Jesus understood that the law could not bring eternal life to this man. If it could then his mission was unnecessary (Gal. 2:21). He was not condemning the man to a life of spiritual bondage and judgment; he was using the law lawfully (1 Tim. 1:8), because the law was good and its purpose was to show that we all need Christ (Rom. 7:12, 16). As Paul said, "Therefore the Law has become our tutor to lead us to Christ, so that we may be justified by faith" (Gal. 3:24).

Jesus recognized that this man needed the humbling that the law provided, which would reveal his own need for the redemption that is only possible with Christ. Unfortunately, we get things backwards. Like the Galatians, we tend to think that grace is for the unbeliever and the law is for the Christian. This is backward. The law is for the unbeliever (1 Tim. 1:8–11); the gospel of grace is for the believer (Rom. 1:8–9).

Often we feel like we have to get people lost before we can get them found. There is some truth to that, not that they are not lost, but that they need to recognize it. Giving people who think they are good enough the gospel of grace doesn't help at all. They need to discover just how much they need Jesus before they will stake their life in him. That is what the law does.

So Jesus took the first commandment—"You shall have no other gods before Me" (Ex. 20:3)—and challenged him with it. "One thing you still lack," he said, "go and sell all that you possess and distribute it to the poor, and you shall have treasure in heaven; and come, follow Me." Jesus summed up that this man had another god—wealth—and that if he surrendered it and followed Jesus, he would step into eternal life. Jesus was not saying that rich people must give up their wealth to be saved. He was also not saying that keeping their wealth was okay either. What he was saying is that we have idols that keep us from following Christ, and we must surrender them.

This is an important story. Is Jesus teaching that an equitable distribution of wealth is the way to salvation? No, I do not think that at all. If that were the case, then he would be teaching us that works are indeed necessary for salvation, which we know is not true. In this story, out of love for the young man, Jesus suggested that he give up the idol that was keeping him in bondage and away from following Christ. Jesus presented the wealthy man with a one-thing spirituality. In fact he summarized, "One thing you lack," and then he instructed the rich man to put aside that which kept him in bondage (put off the old), and follow Jesus (put on the new).

There is, however, a lesson here about the distribution of wealth. The advice Jesus gave the young man was not just to get rid of the idol but specifically to give it to the poor. There is a huge and growing disparity between the grotesque wealth of the super rich and the rapidly declining amount of money in the middle and lower classes of the world. Jesus is commenting on this in at least a backhanded way. You cannot argue that Jesus was a socialist, but you certainly can see how he was interested in helping the poor *and* the rich at the same time—by encouraging the wealthy to give away much of their wealth. To Jesus, money was not a god but simply a tool. It is more important to have generosity than to have wealth. In a spiritual dimension, generosity may indeed be a better security to bank on than riches. This seems to be a constant in the teachings of the revolutionary, Jesus. So Jesus instructed the young man to surrender the idol that he had come to trust in so that he could now put all of his trust in Jesus and "store up . . . treasures in heaven, where neither moth nor rust destroys" (Matt. 6:20).

This was too much for the rich young ruler to swallow, so he walked away dejected. In Mark's gospel, the writer goes out of his way to say that Jesus really loved the man (Mark 10:21). But that didn't cause Jesus to stop him from leaving or to shout out after him, "Hey, when you are ready, it isn't actually the law that will save you, but the gospel." He let him walk away, sad and thinking.

Jesus then commented on the situation: "How hard it is for those who are wealthy to enter the kingdom of God (Luke 18:24). "It is easier for a camel to go through the eye of a needle than for a rich man to enter the kingdom of God!" (Mark 10:25).

What we discover is that Jesus was concerned with whatever was keeping people from the kingdom of God and eternal life. For rich people, often that is the idol of wealth. This is not a condemnation of wealth or a commentary on socialism. It is simply a statement regarding the condition of a person's soul and concern for that soul.

Is it possible for a rich man to enter the kingdom of heaven? Jesus answered that question next, because the disciples asked it. He said, "With people it is impossible, but not with God; for all things are possible with God" (Mark 10:27). In other words, only by God's grace was it possible to have eternal life.

It is possible for wealthy people to come to Christ, but only with God's grace. The same is true for people without wealth. But wealth is indeed a challenging obstacle to overcome for someone to surrender his or her life and put trust in Christ. It will be more rare to see wealthy people surrender to following Christ than poorer people. This is just the reality of the challenge.

What is more rare is that those people die as wealthy as when they entered the kingdom. History is full of wealthy people entering the kingdom of God, but those same people often die without the same wealth (at least in any earthly bank account). Paul, Barnabas, Francis of Assisi, Nikolaus Zinzendorf, the list of rich people throughout history dying with wealth in heaven and none left on earth is impressive. I've listed only a few, but there have been many.

Someone I know who made millions in business before he turned his life around said, "I want my last check to bounce." Once you surrender the idol that is between you and God, then following Christ is easier in that moment.

William Borden was an heir to wealth made in silver mining, but after coming to Christ in the Moody Church of Chicago, he went to the mission field instead. He renounced his wealth in favor of following Christ to the mission field in northern China. His father was furious at him for "investing" his life this way and cut him off from any possible employment in the family business. Shortly after arriving in Africa for training, William died of meningitis and never made it to his desired destination. His family found the following note in his journal:

No reserve. No retreat. No regrets.

William Borden had found a treasure that could not be taken away. He released any other treasure to gain it. The rich young ruler left the real treasure behind because he could only hold one treasure in his hands. He chose the wrong one. You cannot serve both God and wealth.

Jesus and Zaccheus

As Jesus approached Jerusalem, a large crowd followed his every move. He had performed many miracles, and many wanted to witness what he might do next. This march culminated with the triumphal entry into Jerusalem.

Others in the region were also hearing that the miracle-working Messiah was coming, so the streets were full of bystanders before the advancing crowd arrived. Jericho was the last main stop before this marching crowd ascended the steep thirty-four-hundred-foot incline over the final fifteen miles to Jerusalem. It made sense to stop in Jericho for the night to rest for the upward trek the next day.

As Jesus and the throngs entered Jericho, the whole city came out to see what was going on. In that chaos, one height-challenged man wanted to get a look at the one called Jesus. He had heard so much about Jesus, but he couldn't see anything but the backs of other onlookers. There was a stirring desperation in Zaccheus to see Jesus.

Zaccheus was a very wealthy man, but he had paid a great price for his riches. He was a chief tax collector. He made his wealth the old-fashioned way—ripping people off—and sold his soul to the devil. As a tax collector, he was hated by everyone. They thought of him as a traitor. He had sold out to the oppressive Roman Empire just to get rich at the expense of his fellow countrymen. Matthew, a former tax collector, described Jesus as accused as a "friend of tax collectors and sinners" (Matt. 11:19). It appears that tax collectors are in a separate category than all the other sinners, and no doubt there was a special place in hell just for them.

As the chief tax collector, Zaccheus was doubly rich, doubly hated, and doubly lonely. This helps to explain his desperation to at least see Jesus, as well as his lack of concern for his appearance. He knew that Matthew, one of Jesus' followers and closest disciples, had once been a colleague. This made Jesus a popular hero among the most hated people of this culture. Jesus inspired Zaccheus, and he was determined to see this hero. So he decided the only way to do so was to climb a tree, and hang out on a branch. This is a very humiliating position to be in, but Zaccheus was already despised. He was desperate enough that he didn't care what anyone else thought.

Finally, he saw Jesus walking toward him with hundreds of people around him. He looked like a very important man, walking with purpose in his step and so many people eager to be close to him. As Jesus was about to pass by, the most amazing thing happened. He stopped, looked up at Zaccheus, and called him by name. He said, "Zaccheus, hurry and come down, for today I must stay at your house" (Luke 19:5).

I imagine Zaccheus almost fell out of the tree. At the same moment, he realized that everyone was suddenly looking at him, and I'm sure the expressions on their faces were not warm and welcoming.

Zaccheus quickly climbed down and came to Jesus. The people were stunned that Jesus would associate with such a nefarious sinner.

With his heart racing, every hair standing at attention, and adrenalin shooting through his body, Zaccheus felt the enormity of this moment. This was not expected at all. He had only wanted to see the face of the man who was a friend of tax collectors. But Jesus was not only friendly, he knew him by name and, in front of all these people, chose to identify with him in as intimate a social setting as possible. How did Jesus even know his name? Perhaps being the chief tax collector had some measure of notoriety. Maybe

Zaccheus had met Jesus at Matthew's party, which he threw after meeting Jesus for the first time (Matt. 9:9–10). It is even possible that Jesus knew his name by prophetic revelation. In any case, to hear Jesus speak his name must have been a powerful and life-changing jolt for Zaccheus. He felt something he hadn't felt in a long time, perhaps even since childhood: hope.

This was more than he could have asked for. He was overcome with gratitude and love, and in that moment, he exclaimed to Jesus, "Behold, Lord, half of my possessions I will give to the poor, and if I have defrauded anyone of anything, I will give back four times as much" (Luke 19:8). All he really needed was a little hope, and he would gladly give everything back. Why not? He had given his life to ill-gotten gains, and they had done nothing for him but seal him into a lonely prison of social outcast.

Whereas the rich young ruler found a sense of identity, power, and purpose in his riches, Zaccheus found only hatred, loneliness, and isolation. It was too hard for the young ruler to give up his wealth, but it was all too easy for Zaccheus. I imagine he felt a great release and freedom at that moment. He completely forgot the crowds around him and could only see Jesus and feel the freedom of finally reconciling the debt he felt in his soul.

In response to Zaccheus's proclamation Jesus made an announcement of his own. He said, "Today salvation has come to this house, because he, too, is a son of Abraham. For the Son of Man has come to seek and to save that which was lost" (Luke 19:9–10).

If Zaccheus felt overwhelmed moments ago, at these words, he must have broken down into sobs. I can't imagine others in the crowd not weeping a bit, too, and more than a few doing the math to figure out how much of Zaccheus's estate they were entitled to. Jesus publicly identified Zaccheus as saved, but more than that, he was now a true child of Abraham and welcomed back into his own people.

With the rich young ruler, Jesus had to broach the topic of generosity. With Zaccheus, Jesus only needed to be friendly and to identify with him, and he volunteered to distribute his wealth with justice and generosity. In both cases, Jesus showed compassion and love for the soul of the wealthy person and seemed to know exactly what was best for that person. He doesn't treat them both the same. However, in both cases, the subject of a generosity toward those who are less fortunate was brought front and center.

Jesus said it clearly, and obviously not just to Zaccheus but to the whole crowd (and to us as well), "The Son of Man has come to seek and to save that which was lost" (Luke 19:10). He didn't come to judge them but to save them. He didn't revolt against the system or even take the political avenues available to him to bring about change. He was interested in saving those who were lost. His advice to give wealth to the poor was motivated more for the soul of the one who would give than those who would receive.

It is clear that Jesus loved the wealthy as much as anyone else, no matter how they came into their wealth. He addressed whatever stumbling block was keeping the wealthy person from the salvation he needed. But we cannot leave these stories without noticing that he did hold the wealthy responsible with their wealth. In fact, while everyone was listening to Jesus under the shade of that sycamore tree, he gave a parable about being faithful with what you have received. Hoarding it or hiding it is not an option. Money is a test of our souls. If we are faithful with the small things—such as money—Jesus will entrust to us greater wealth. But if it takes over our souls, we fail the test.

One of these wealthy men passed the test and one did not. One found true riches; the other did not. When we encounter Jesus, it must affect our hearts. You cannot follow Jesus and remain selfish. You cannot follow Jesus and continue following mammon. One thing is clear in these gospel stories: Jesus will affect your bank account if you take him to heart and start to follow him. If you have accepted Jesus, but your financial practices have not altered or changed in any way, then you likely need to reevaluate your faith.

THE FISCAL GAP IN JESUS' JOURNEY TO JERUSALEM . . . AND THE CROSS

In Luke's gospel, sandwiched conspicuously between the rich young ruler and Zaccheus, is the story of the blind beggar Bartimaeus (Luke 18:35–43). As the parade of people following Jesus to Jericho and ultimately Jerusalem progressed along the Jordan River Valley, a voice cried out: "Jesus, son of David, have mercy on me!" (Luke 18:38).

All the people who found a sense of importance in being close to Jesus scolded the beggar for bothering this important person. But the man shouted all the louder. This was his only chance, his only hope. He had nothing to lose and everything to gain.

Jesus heard the calls, stopped, and had the people who had just scolded the beggar bring the man to him. He asked Bartimaeus, "What do you want Me to do for you?" (v. 41).

Jesus was a servant to all, rich and poor alike. All the people in this posse felt they were more important than the blind beggar on the side of the road. Really, the only person who we can argue is more important is the only one who thought the needs and desires of the beggar were more important than his own. So he paused and had the man brought to him and asked the beggar what he could do for him.

The man said, "Lord, I want to regain my sight!" Jesus replied, "Receive your sight; your faith has made you well" (vv. 41–42). And with that the man was healed and began to follow Jesus to Jericho, Jerusalem, Golgotha, and the resurrection.

Bartimaeus and Zaccheus likely shared a meal together, and perhaps a whole lot more than that. There is a reason why Luke gives us their names but we only get a description of the rich young ruler.

Bartimaeus and Zaccheus became family and are known. The gap was closed because of the love birthed by the good news of Jesus Christ. The poor were empowered and the rich were, too, but while their salvation was the same, the way it played out in their financial standings was quite different.

The rich young ruler, however, is never mentioned again, forgotten except for this story recorded three times in the New Testament for all to read. He is likely grateful that we do not know his name.

As Paul pointed out, "God shows no partiality" (Gal. 2:6). We do not impress God with our status or position in life; he sees us all the same. When Jesus looks at a rich person, he sees a person he loves. When he looks at a poor person, he sees a person he loves. He isn't impressed by wealth, and he isn't shocked by poverty. He sees through such things to a person's heart. If only we could do the same.

Jesus encountered three people. A rich man left Jesus' company grieved with nothing more than he had before. A poor man became richer and empowered. Another rich man became poorer and was restored.

Jesus looks upon everyone with love and sees them as unique. He seeks and saves any who are broken and blind, but he always gives them a choice to follow him or not.

How are we to apply Jesus' view of money in our lives? We must not ascribe significant value to money. We must see it as a tool and know that it would be a terrible master. If we would view money as Jesus did, we would live simpler lives and sacrificial lives. We would be less consumed with getting it, saving it, spending it, or increasing it. We would be more content with enough and not driven for more.

In the next chapter we will watch how Jesus responded to the poor. We will again look at two stories of different people bound together by the Scriptures to teach us that the poor need to be responsive but can be just as irresponsible if they choose to.

Chapter 8

JESUS TAKES ON WELFARE

Love means loving the unlovable, or it is no virtue at all.
— G. K. CHESTERTON

The bread which you hold back belongs to the hungry;
the coat, which you guard in your locked storage-chest
belongs to the naked; the footwear mouldering in your
closet belongs to those without shoes. The silver that you
keep hidden in a safe place belongs to the one in need.
— SAINT BASIL THE GREAT

There are many accounts of Jesus' encounters with poor people; in fact, it's the very heart of his mission. In his first public appearance, he read the following text from Isaiah and claimed it for himself as a way of announcing his arrival:

> The Spirit of the Lord is upon Me,
> Because He anointed Me to preach the gospel to the
> poor.
> He has sent Me to proclaim release to the captives,

And recovery of sight to the blind,
To set free those who are oppressed,
To proclaim the favorable year of the Lord.
(Luke 4:18–21)

That sounds like a revolutionary. Jesus' mission was to set the captives free and bring good news to those who are under the heavy weight of poverty. Christians, it is time that we recognize our Savior and acknowledge that he is a revolutionary.

For a more holistic view, I will discuss two of the Lord's encounters with the poor: the man born blind and the lame man at the pool of Bethesda. As in the previous chapter, we will see how Jesus responded differently to both men, despite many similarities. In fact, like the previous chapter, I believe these two stories are meant to be compared in order to teach us much, so we will look at both the surprising similarities and the glaring differences.

JESUS WITH THE POOLSIDE PARALYTIC

Skeptics of divine healers today tend to ask the same question: If you really do have the gift of healing, why don't you go where the sick people are, like a hospital, instead of asking everyone to come to your church service? That is a legitimate question. We find Jesus does, indeed, go where sick people are, and he doesn't have any Sunday church services and never takes an offering. In John 5:1–18 we find Jesus doing just that. In his time, there was a pool called the pool of Bethesda. Legend had it that every now and then an angel would stir up the waters, and whoever was first to touch the water afterward would be healed. So sick people surrounded the pool, waiting for their moment. It was there, where the sick people were, that Jesus came to perform a miracle.

Stepping over many of the sick, Jesus found a man who had been paralyzed for thirty-eight years and asked him an obvious question: "Do you wish to get well?" (v. 6). The man is at the pool of Bethesda, which means pool of mercy, waiting for the stirring of the water. Wouldn't one assume that he wants to be well? We might, but Jesus knew better.

This is a profoundly important question to ask. As he did with the rich young ruler, Jesus began this encounter with a question suited specifically for the core spiritual problem of the individual. We should all learn to ask this question more frequently. Many who complain about their lot in life would rather not be healed if it means having to give up the addictive lifestyle that brought about the devastation in their life. As we will see, such was the case in this story.

The man's response was indicative of someone who lives in dysfunction and is unwilling to address the true problem. That is, he blames everyone else. He said, "Sir, I have no man to put me into the pool when the water is stirred up, but while I am coming, another steps down before me" (v. 7). He blamed other people for not helping him enough. He blamed other people for stepping into the pool before him. In fact, the only one who seemed to skirt his blame game was himself. Once again, Jesus accurately summed up a person's spiritual problems in short order.

Without correcting the man or taking the conversation any further, Jesus healed him. He commanded him to stand, pick up his bedding, and walk. Immediately the man was healed. And Jesus disappeared into the crowd.

All of this happened on a Saturday, the Sabbath, and as the healed man was walking and carrying his bed, he was at once in trouble with the religious leaders. They scolded him for carrying something on the Sabbath. The man's response was consistent with his pattern: he blamed another. He said, "He who made me well was the one who said to me, 'Pick up your pallet and walk'" (v. 11).

I don't know which is more flabbergasting: the religious leaders or the man who was healed. A man who had been paralyzed for thirty-eight years had been instantly healed and was walking about, but all the religious leaders can see is that nothing like this is supposed to happen on the Sabbath. At the same time, the man who had suffered for thirty-eight years and who had been completely healed in a moment just threw his healer under the bus to save his own butt.

The religious leaders, smelling an even worse culprit, who not only tells others to carry things on the Sabbath but heals on the Sabbath as well, inquire who the healer was. But the man doesn't know. He can't answer their question.

Later, Jesus found the man and had a few words with him. First, Jesus pointed to the fact that the man could now walk, showing him the mercy he has received and waking him up to the truly incredible gift of healing. He said, "Do not sin anymore, so that nothing worse happens to you" (v. 14). What is worse than thirty-eight years of paralysis? Well, thirty-nine years of paralysis is indeed worse. Actually, I suspect death is the next consequence, though we can't know for sure. What we can know is that it is not going to be good. It is going to be worse than the condition the man lived in prior to being healed by Jesus, and that cannot be a good thing.

We learn something from this dialogue that informs us about all that preceded the healing. The man was paralyzed because of self-destructive patterns in his life. This was a crucible moment for him. All of his life led up to this moment, and the outcome would be as different as heaven and hell for him. He could put aside his sin and choose to follow Christ or he could continue down the path he had been on and suffer a terrible end.

How did the man respond to this significant moment? He went to find the Pharisees so he could tell them it was Jesus' fault for violating the Sabbath, not his. Rather than admit his responsibility for his tragic life, he found someone else to blame. He also made Jesus' life harder afterward, as John tells us, "For this reason therefore the Jews were seeking all the more to kill Him" (v. 18).

The former paralytic was a man with such self-destructive patterns in his life that he ended up completely dependent on others for his every need for thirty-eight years. Someone had to carry him to the pool each day and pick him up later. He could eat only because of the kindness of others. His life was empty because he did nothing but lay around all day and hope someone would eventually help him. But when someone helped him beyond any hope in the world, he turned on his benefactor for his own selfish gain.

So how did Jesus treat this welfare recipient? He did all he could to empower this person to make the right decision. He first asked him if he truly wanted to get well. The answer he received was less than stellar; nevertheless, Jesus healed him. Jesus' grace and mercy were not dependent on people's responding correctly.

Perhaps Jesus asked the first question because he knew the answer and was hoping the paralytic would discover it. Perhaps the paralytic actually didn't want to get well, preferring to live on the care and constant support of others. Perhaps Jesus robbed him of that excuse, and for that reason he identified Jesus to the religious authorities. Much of this is speculation. Based on Jesus' first question and the response of the man, though, it is not speculation without justification.

Later, Jesus searched for the man to warn him of the impending consequences of continuing in his destructive lifestyle. His warning seemed not to have helped the man. Jesus did everything he could to help, but ultimately we all have to bear responsibility for our decisions in life. Even when the man was at a disadvantage because of his own mistakes, Jesus still gave him a leg up to help. Then, reminding him of his new opportunity, he warned him clearly. But he still empowered the man to make his own decisions and live (or die) with the consequences.

From the first response, the paralytic demonstrated he was unworthy of a miracle and deserved his plight. If we had had the power to heal the man, many of us would have walked away and left him in the midst of his mess of a life. But Jesus didn't. He healed him when the man did not deserve it, ask for it, or even believe in it. Did Jesus waste a miracle? Was Jesus being irresponsible by giving such a gift to such an undeserving soul? Didn't Jesus know this man would likely not turn his life around?

The name of the pool meant pool of mercy, not pool of "you get what you deserve."

When we debate issues of social justice, welfare, and caring for the poor and downtrodden, we can easily find excuses not to care. This is a condemnation on us as followers of Jesus. His miracles were not just for those who deserved it. The theological definition of *grace* is "unmerited favor." By its very definition, grace is for people who do not deserve it. We follow the God of all mercy, and we should be characterized as a people of mercy. Welfare is meant to provide some benefit to those who are incapable of helping themselves. It is grace. Jesus provided a lift to someone who needed it even if he didn't deserve it, ask for it, or even appreciate it. Jesus gave him a hand up not a handout.

My friend Dezi Baker said that we should strive to save people in every way they can be saved. Doesn't that sound like a mission deserving of Jesus?

Jesus said:

But when the Son of Man comes in His glory, and all the angels with Him, then He will sit on His glorious throne. All the nations will be gathered before Him; and He will separate them from one another, as the shepherd separates the sheep from the goats; and He will put the sheep on His right, and the goats on the left.

Then the King will say to those on His right, "Come, you who are blessed of My Father, inherit the kingdom prepared for you from the foundation of the world. For I was hungry, and you gave Me something to eat; I was thirsty, and you gave Me something to drink; I was a stranger, and you invited Me in; naked, and you clothed Me; I was sick, and you visited Me; I was in prison, and you came to Me." Then the righteous will answer Him, "Lord, when did we see You hungry, and feed You, or thirsty, and give You something to drink? And when did we see You a stranger, and invite You in, or naked, and clothe You? When did we see You sick, or in prison, and come to You?" The King will answer and say to them, "Truly I say to you, to the extent that you did it to one of these brothers of Mine, even the least of them, you did it to Me." (Matt. 25:31–40)

Why are we so content to only enlist people in heaven and church membership when we can enlist them to the kingdom right now, in a world that needs it? Why would those who are to be identified by love not want to lift people from the gutter? We should give them the good news of eternal life in the hereafter and in the here and now.

With empowerment comes responsibility. This is not just a slogan from the Spider-Man movies. Of course, to empower people we need to give them responsibility for their lives, and some will not respond well to that. Like the poolside paralytic, some will only want others to take responsibility for their lives, and these will only know destruction.

Blame shifting, excuse making, covering up, and justification for sin are the fruit of someone who is unwilling to change. Such is often the case with those who are at the end of their rope because of repeated patterns of sin and destruction. These people always hurt more people than themselves. They put the heavy burden of their dysfunction on everyone else and cause the most pain to those who love them. The world has always had plenty of people like this, and I am sure you know people like this as well.

We can assume that when worse things indeed happened to the former paralytic because of a lack of change in his lifestyle, Jesus did not perform more miracles to heal him again and again. This seems likely a one-time deal with a very heavy warning. What the former paralytic did with it was completely his responsibility.

JESUS WITH THE MAN BORN BLIND

On another Sabbath day, Jesus and his disciples were walking through Jerusalem and came across a man who had been born blind. The disciples asked Jesus, "Rabbi, who sinned, this man [in the womb is implied] or his parents, that he would be born blind?"

(John 9:2). Of course their real question was, "Is it fair that God should have this man suffer all his life for the sins of his parents or, worse, some sin he could commit in the womb?"

Jesus answered with a remarkable revelation. In essence, he said that it wasn't for sin that the man had been born blind but for the present moment. Then Jesus did the strangest thing. Which is worse, someone putting dirt in your eyes or spitting in your eyes? The answer is "all the above." Jesus spat on the ground, scooped up the muddy saliva, and smeared it on the eyes of this unsuspecting man. (I often wonder, was Jesus a good spitter? You know some people are real good at spitting with velocity and accuracy. Did the saliva shoot from his mouth or did it drop and hang for a while before finally hitting the ground? Either way, he likely had to wipe spit from his beard. I honestly don't know if he was well practiced at spitting or not.)

Picture Jesus spitting on the ground, stirring the mud with his fingers, scooping it up, and turning to the blind man sitting on his mat with his useless eyes wide open. The blind man didn't see what was happening. Then Jesus smeared the mud on the man's eyes. What a sight this must have been. Bibles should carry a warning label at this portion of Scripture: Warning, Do Not Try This at Home.

Jesus then told the blind man, "Go, wash in the pool of Siloam" (v. 7). And the man obeyed. John tells us that Siloam means "sent." The blind man didn't know Jesus and had never read a book, but he responded when the Lord sent him on a mission.

In this instance, the man did not ask to be healed or saved. Jesus took the initiative and did so in a rather unorthodox if not rude manner. Without even introducing himself, Jesus rubbed the man's sightless eyes with mud made from his spit!

The blind man obeyed Jesus, which demonstrated at least some measure of faith. Of course, why wouldn't he want to wash his face with the saliva and mud on his eyes? And he was healed as a result of this small act of faith.

Again, a Sabbath miracle created quite a stir in the city. Everyone was questioning if this was indeed the man who had been born blind. And he said with glee, "I am the one" (v. 9). He wanted to tell the world what Jesus had done for him. He wasn't shy about it. This was the best thing that had ever happened to him, and he wanted to tell everyone. Of course, the people gave him his day in court. They took him to the Pharisees.

In the ensuing legal proceeding, we watch as the seeing man became just that: a man who sees. Watch his emerging faith and conviction grow in the heat of examination and debate. To me, this is one of the most beautiful stories in the Bible.

The Pharisees launched an inquiry into this event because, in their eyes, a law had been broken—the Sabbath law. Oddly enough, they were not the slightest bit amazed by the miracle standing in front of them. All they could see was that their petty rules had been broken. All such infractions were punishable by stoning.

A debate ensued among the Pharisees over whether a sinner could perform such miracles or not. But in the midst of this discussion, the Pharisees made a mistake. They asked the seeing man what he thought of this Jesus. His answer came without hesitation, "He is a prophet" (v. 17).

The Jewish leaders couldn't accept this conclusion, so they began a ridiculous pursuit—to refute that this man had been born blind. They wouldn't accept the evidence in front of them, so they called for testimony from other eyewitnesses. First, they called his parents to the stand. Fearing the decree that had already gone out that if any would confess Jesus as the Christ, he or she would be excommunicated from the synagogue, the man's parents simply identified him as their son and confirmed that he had been born blind. As to how he could see now, they did not venture to answer but referred to their son, who was old enough to speak for himself. That got the Pharisees back to square one.

Getting frustrated by a lack of progress, the religious leaders turned again to the seeing man and said, "Give glory to God; we know that this man is a sinner" (v. 24). So many people tragically spend their lives justifying false presuppositions and never learn anything. Like these religious leaders, they can look a miracle in the eye and see only their own petty rules and regulations.

It is interesting that Jesus declared at the beginning of this story that this man was born to give glory to God, which is exactly what the religious leaders demanded he do. And he did by demonstrating this miraculous work for all to see. Ironically, the man was, in fact, fulfilling the Pharisees' request when he acknowledged the miracle Jesus had done.

While the Pharisees were appealing for him to give the credit to God and not to this sinner named Jesus, the seeing man declared an irrefutable argument on behalf of his newly emerging faith. He said, "Whether He is a sinner, I do not know; one thing I do know, that though I was blind, now I see" (v. 25). The seeing man under the spotlight of interrogation had stumbled into a one-thing spiritual awakening.

The Pharisees had no recourse. They could spout theology and pious statements of condemnation, but they couldn't challenge this simple statement of faith coming from a man who knew next to nothing about Jesus. The man was not an expert about the law, theology, or the identity of the Messiah, but the one thing he was qualified to be an expert on was his own experience. No one could challenge this.

Out of frustration, they asked the seeing man once more how Jesus performed the miracle. By now the man was weary of this proceeding, and he was beginning to see that these religious men didn't have any answer to his statement. This gave him a growing sense of confidence. These men were not so untouchable. When they asked yet again how the miracle happened, he began to exert some of his strength and a bit of good old-fashioned sarcasm. He said, "I told you already and you did not listen; why do you want to hear it again? You do not want to become His disciples too, do you?" (v. 27).

Confronted with this strong, uneducated witness who couldn't even read, the Pharisees began to feel threatened and reacted with the usual condemnation of an opponent and a recital of their religious credentials for being right. They pronounced what they considered to be a grave accusation meant to hurt him, but which is in reality the greatest compliment the seeing man had ever received. They said, "You are His disciple, but we are disciples of Moses" (v. 28). Then they spouted more theology and said, "We know that God has spoken to Moses, but as for this man, we do not know where He is from" (v. 29).

At this point the seeing man felt a great release. He had never thought of himself as a disciple of anyone. Until this moment he had been an outcast, a loser, an obvious sinner punished by God. Now he was a disciple of Jesus! I don't think he even thought of such a possibility until his highly tuned ears heard it for the first time from his accusers, who happened to be the religious experts of the land. He didn't even know Jesus, but suddenly he was a disciple of this man whom everyone talked about. He felt a little bolder, a little more confident of his position. The Pharisees had fallen unsuspectingly into a trap when they acclaimed their master (Moses) as better than his (Jesus).

With new boldness that came from identifying with Jesus, the man took the initiative. He went on the offense against the invincible Pharisees! Without waiting to be asked anything more, he said,

> Well, here is an amazing thing, that you do not know where He is from, and yet He opened my eyes. We know that God does not hear sinners; but if anyone is God-fearing and does His will, He hears him. Since the beginning of time it has never been heard that anyone opened the eyes of a person born blind. If this man were not from God, He could do nothing. (vv. 30–33)

The Pharisees never liked it when they were told they didn't know something, so this was a real insult.

The seeing man was beginning to see even more clearly. He suddenly began to understand that Jesus was greater than these hypocritical Jewish leaders. They played the "my master is better than your master" game by comparing Moses with Jesus, and now the seeing man had expounded on something of which he was an expert—the healing of people born blind. Not even Moses was able to do that! No one, "since the beginning of time," had been able to do that. Checkmate!

But this move further offended the Pharisees, who had no argument except to again resort to condemnation and propound the superiority of their position in life. They brought the story full circle to the original assumption behind the question (which the now-seeing man had probably heard), "Who sinned, this man or his parents?" They said, "You were born entirely in sins, and are you teaching us?" (v. 34). And with that, the blind Pharisees excommunicated the seeing man.

Even this last attempt at criticizing and condemning the seeing man was a backhanded compliment. Just think of it; only a few hours earlier, he was a blind man with no hope and no respect, begging on the streets for some food. All who saw him assumed him to be a wretched sinner, for otherwise God wouldn't have made him blind. Now, after a brief encounter with this mysterious man known as Jesus, he was standing before great and educated Pharisees as they admitted *he* was teaching *them*! He was teaching them theology. His teaching was not only sound, but his argument won the debate. Their attempt to label him as one born entirely in sins only encouraged him more, because Jesus had already proven, irrefutably, that he had not been born blind because of his sins. He could see! There was no evidence that he was born entirely in his sins, as was once thought, at least not any more than anyone else. No, the ones who evidenced blindness and bondage to sin were the Pharisees, not this man.

A question begs to be asked: *Why did Jesus choose to perform this miracle in such a strange way?* In fact, Jesus told us why at the very beginning. He said this man had been born blind "so that the works of God might be displayed in him" (John 9:3). Jesus healed him in a delayed fashion (by not accompanying him to the pool) so that the seeing man could be brought alone to the Pharisees, and Jesus would not be the one defending his actions. I believe Jesus wanted the man to stand before the Pharisees since he had never even seen Jesus, knew little about him, and yet would refute and embarrass them. In the course of the man's debate with the Pharisees, he was able to identify Jesus as a prophet from God who performed miracles that no one had ever done in all of history, not even Moses. Jesus had already gotten the best of the Pharisees, but when an uneducated, formerly blind beggar and obvious (to them) sinner did so, God received even greater glory for the miracle of a changed life.

It's fascinating to note that just a short time earlier, Jesus had debated with these same Pharisees, and they had rebuked him: "You are testifying about Yourself; Your testimony is not true" (John 8:13). Jesus responded in two ways. He said, "Even if I testify about Myself, My testimony is true, for I know where I came from and where I am going; but you do not know where I come from or where I am going" (v. 14).

The second thing he did was to send the healed blind man as a witness to defend where he came from. And he defended Jesus admirably. We often think we need to send our most knowledgeable and intelligent people to witness to the world. We think our education and philosophical arguments will convince people of Jesus' divinity. The truth is that the most persuasive and effective argument for the validity of Jesus' claims is the testimony of a changed life. This powerful ammunition is given to any and all who follow him. It doesn't require a high IQ, degrees, or high position in life. Any one of us, no, *every one* of us possesses this potential.

We also tend to think that if a famous, successful person becomes a Christian, he or she will be a more effective witness because of all they have to offer the kingdom. There is a theological word to describe this point of view: *hogwash*. The kingdom has much to offer all that come to Christ; it doesn't need anything from the world.

In fact, the most destitute and broken people who are changed by Jesus become the greatest witnesses of God's power. In the Gospels, Jesus doesn't wait for despicable people to become mature saints before he unleashes their powerful testimonies on others.

Remember the Samaritan woman at the well (John 4:28–30, 39–42)? What about the Gerasene demoniac set free and commissioned to stay behind (Mark 5:1–20)? Do you find it amazing that Matthew was a despised tax collector in one scene (Matt. 9:9), hosted an evangelistic outreach party in the next (vv. 10–13), and then was sent into the cities as an apostle to preach the gospel just a few verses later (10:1–8)?

A third reason Jesus healed in this fashion is that he was a revolutionary, and he was not one to succumb to the false systems of law imposed on people by self-righteous leaders. He not only did miracles on the Sabbath, but he also broke the oral traditions of the elders of Israel, known as the Talmud, when he healed in this way. Because of an association to pagan magic, certain rabbis prohibited the use of saliva to heal someone.[1] The traditions of the religious leaders forbade healing on the Sabbath, the making of clay on the Sabbath, and even placing spit on eyelids.[2] Yes, Jesus was a radical revolutionary who rebelled against the status quo any chance he could. He came to change the world, and that required bucking the system in overt ways.

COMPARING AND CONTRASTING BOTH STORIES

I believe these two stories, just like the two stories about rich men in Luke's gospel, are supposed to be compared. They tell a story together that needs to be told. The story of each is incomplete without the other. Below are the similarities and the differences in these stories. I list them here to show the overwhelming evidence that they are meant to be compared.

Story Similarities

- Jesus approached the person healed.
- Jesus initiated the conversation.
- The question of sin's cause for the illness was raised.
- The one healed was poor and dependent on the kindness of others.
- The miracle took place on the Sabbath.
- The one healed didn't ask to be healed or expect it.
- The one healed did not know who Jesus was until afterward.
- Both people were afflicted for a long time.
- A pool was involved with both, and the name of the pool was meaningful to the story.
- The one healed didn't believe in Jesus when he was healed.
- Jesus disappeared immediately before/after the miracle.
- Attention was on the one healed, not the healer.
- A miracle occurred, but the religious leaders could only see that the Sabbath had been violated.
- The religious leaders interrogated the one healed afterward.
- After the man was interrogated by the religious leaders, Jesus found him to follow up.

Story Differences

- One was sick because of sin; the other was not.
- One took responsibility for his new opportunity; the other would not.
- One showed great gratitude; the other did not.
- One exalted Christ's name; the other made Jesus' work harder.
- One resisted the Pharisees; the other kowtowed to them.
- One followed Christ; the other did not.

- One would have a better life; the other's life would get worse and likely ended badly.

Though there are more similarities, we can learn more from the differences. We see that some are more receptive to mercy and miracles than others. Just because someone is poor and dependent upon others does not mean he or she will turn things around if given a lift. Some will; others will not. But the results of their decisions should not dictate our love and mercy. We do not react based on their response or worthiness; our love and mercy should be consistent and constant regardless of how others respond to it. Giving grace to those who do not deserve it and may not even appreciate it is part of what grace is. We should go out of our way to give grace to others, even if that means wasting it. That's what Jesus did, and that is what we are called to do.

The Old Testament law spelled out different ways we are to provide help for those who are unable to help themselves. This shows us that God indeed desires us to provide assistance to people in need. Even at times when a person's indebtedness is self-inflicted, the law still provided assistance and ultimate freedom. In either case, empowering people by giving them a choice to do better and allowing them the responsibility for their decisions are a must.

Frankly, the church of Jesus should be providing welfare for all who are unable to care for themselves. In the absence of that, we have governments stepping in to do it. This is a poor option at best and an indictment on the church at worst, but it may be all there is for some people. I truly believe that if the church in the United States were alive with faith working through love, many government programs would never have been conceived or implemented.

If every church took responsibility to care for just two foster kids, there would no longer be a foster care system in the US. You can hardly find a more redundant command in all of Scripture than caring for orphans. Yet, like so many other needs we ignore, caring for orphans is left to our government.

At times when the church was alive, hospitals were created, schools were created, slavery was abolished, women received the right to vote, alcoholism was reduced, even prisons became obsolete during the Welsh revival. Instead, the government is so big because the church is so small. In a sense, the government is in such places because the church isn't. Instead of complaining about someone doing what we should be doing, we should start living out what we say we believe. Stop griping and protesting, and start loving and giving generously.

It is unfortunate that for a long time the church has been consumed with its own wants and desires. Prior to the 2009 financial crisis, the church was spending $70 billion every decade on buildings alone. That figure has dropped a little, but it is still too high. If you throw in salaries for staff members, the amount we spend on ourselves is overwhelming, and all our income and spending are tax free. We can't care for others because we are too busy caring for ourselves. And the world knows it.

What Jesus showed us in these two stories is that we should offer assistance even when the recipients are not expecting it, asking for it, or even deserving of it. We also must bring empowerment to make people's lives better. What we cannot do is force them to accept responsibility. We can only allow them to face the consequences of their actions after we have done everything we can to help them to make right decisions.

Chapter 9

JESUS TAKES ON WOMEN IN CRISIS

Christians are routinely taught by example and word that
it is more important to be right than it is to be Christ-like.
In fact, being right licenses you to be mean, and, indeed
requires you to be mean—righteously mean, of course.
— DALLAS WILLARD

Martin Luther King gets to call himself a Christian
because he actually practiced loving his enemies.
— BILL MAHER

Women have to endure a lot. They have to live in a world where half the population is men.

Having raised two beautiful daughters, I sometimes get a little ticked off at the way men are. I hate it when men let their eyes focus where they shouldn't for longer than they should. I have been offended by old men who flirt. I've been known to be protective and even embarrass my girls more than a few times in the process. Whenever a young man calls me "sir," I tell him the only person

I let call me "sir" is anyone who is dating my daughter. Yeah, I can be a little protective. So can their brother. My son-in-law can vouch for that. He's a beloved part of the family now, but he had to endure a lot to earn it.

One time my daughter and I were crossing a street in front of a car, and two young men hooted at my daughter. When I looked back at them, they shouted an offensive remark before they drove off. The fools then pulled into a fast-food drive-through no more than fifty feet away.

I couldn't help myself. I was so outraged on behalf of my daughter that I had to do something. I waited until they were boxed in, with a car in front and another behind them. I then walked toward the car's passenger side. I saw that they were smoking pot and laughing, full of brazen male cockiness, but not for long.

I slammed my hand on the roof of the car over their heads and loudly yelled into the open passenger window, "Hey!"

They jumped so high their heads hit the ceiling of the car. I think the airbags almost deployed. You could see fear in their eyes, whereas back at the crosswalk they yelled defiantly at me, "Yeah, we're looking at your daughter's—." Not only did the noise scare them, but now a crazy dude (who is no little man) had them trapped. All their cockiness was immediately gone.

The passenger was fumbling to pick up the lit joint that had fallen in his lap and was starting to burn a hole in his pants and anything under the fabric. The other started to mumble lame excuses and apologies, none of which were intelligible as he looked around to confirm that he couldn't just drive away.

I paused for a while, taking it all in with a smirk. I looked at the two of them in their humiliation with a look of disgust and said, "Real classy, guys. You must impress the ladies." I shook my head and said again, "Real classy." Then I walked away, letting them wallow in their humiliation.

Men are pigs—99.5 percent of the time. And women have to deal with it all the time. In fact, women often pay the price for guys being ugly men. Sorry guys, this is our reality, and I am a man, so I can say it. Why do you think it is that fathers are so protective of their daughters when young men come to court? Men know about men. And women do too, but young girls may still be naive about the dark side of the male gender.

This little story is nothing. All over the world women are not just being embarrassed by men; they are being abused, used, and spat out. In many places of the world, women are raped and then killed as punishment for adultery as so-called honor killings. Young women are stolen and then sold against their will to become wives or trafficked in the sex industry. Much of the world denies them a basic education. They are not allowed a voice in their society. Often they cannot drive a car or vote in an election. And in many parts of the world they are forced to live in a burka. Why? Because men are pigs. Women are not perfect by any means, but men are idiots, and women have to pay the price for the evil that men do.

This is nothing new. In Jesus' time, women were used and abused. In this chapter we will look at two encounters recorded in John's gospel that show how Jesus responded to women who were exploited by men. While neither of the women was completely innocent, they nonetheless had to pay a much bigger price for their sexuality than men. This is seemingly always the case. In this chapter we will see how Jesus addressed two women paying a shameful price for the blunt end of men's sexual drive, and both stories come from chapters 4 and 8 of the gospel of John.

THE WOMAN AT THE WELL

After a long day of walking, Jesus was tired, hungry, and thirsty. He and the disciples stopped at a place where good Jews would never be found. They were walking from Judea to Galilee, and they stopped in the Samaritan village of Sychar. At this site is a famous well of Jacob, so Jesus paused here while the disciples went to town to get food.

Normally Jews going between Galilee and Judea avoided Samaria entirely, walking many miles out of their way around the land. Why would they take the long route to avoid this place? Because it was inhabited by heretical half-breeds—Samaritans.

When Jesus wanted to teach a lesson about what a true neighbor is like, he told the story of the good Samaritan. This was outlandish because Jews did not consider Samaritans to be good in any way. At another time the Lord and his disciples were passing through Samaria and needed a place to spend the night, but they were turned away by a Samaritan innkeeper. James and John suggested they pray for fire to fall from heaven and destroy the Samaritans. Needless to say, Jews hated Samaritans. But Jesus loved them.

In the midday sun, a Samaritan woman descended alone from the village, carrying her water pot to the well. Usually women drew water in the early, cooler morning hours. This woman found it better to do so in the draining heat of midday, when no one else would be around. Her plans to be alone, however, were disrupted by Jesus.

She tried to ignore him, going about the task of drawing water from the well. But Jesus would not allow that. "Give Me a drink," he said (v. 7).

Just speaking to her broke every social and cultural taboo imaginable. Jesus was a man; she was a woman. Jesus was a Jew;

she was a Samaritan. While she may not have known this yet, he was a holy man, a rabbi, and she was a woman of possible poor reputation. There was every reason not to speak to her, but he did. Jesus felt no such cultural or spiritual restrictions.

She was so shocked that she never actually responded to him, only to the social convention that was obliterated. She might have had suspicions about his intentions. Why not? Men were always approaching women with less than wholesome intentions. In fact, the way the world worked, it was almost a given that every thought a man had around a woman when they were alone was only sexual. That was what everything in her experience told her. She had been used by men over and over. And she had used men as well. That is the nature of things. Why should this moment and this man be any different from the others?

Since they were alone, perhaps she suspected he could break more than few religious taboos and no one would ever know. It was as if he asked her, "Can I buy you a drink?" Rather than indulge the potential proposition she suspected was coming, she asked the obvious question to change the subject. While this is mere specu-lation, it is certainly a viable assumption. It is also possible that she sensed Jesus' love and felt safe. In either case, he shattered all cultural taboos, and the woman was certainly more than a little curious.

She said, "How is it that You, being a Jew, ask me for a drink since I am a Samaritan woman?" (v. 9).

The next thing Jesus said to her is flat-out comical in com-parison to her possible suspicions. He said, "If you knew the gift of God, and who it is who says to you, 'Give Me a drink,' you would have asked Him, and He would have given you living water" (v. 10).

If that didn't confirm her suspicions, I don't know what possibly would. What she heard was, *He thinks he is a gift from God to women and that I should be asking him for a drink! Geez, men can be so full of themselves!* Her next thought was likely, *I wish I could humiliate this man, but I don't know him. He could be dangerous. I better be careful how I respond to this weirdo since there are no witnesses.* It is unfortunate, but more often than you might think, women have to think thoughts like this.

This part of the conversation rolls out like a scene from a comedy where an egotistical guy is hitting on a beautiful woman, and she keeps deflecting his comments and shooting him down while trying to bring things back to earth. It wouldn't stay on earth for long though, because she had no idea who it was she was really talking to or what his pure intentions actually were.

Stating the obvious, "Sir," the woman said, "You have nothing to draw with and the well is deep; where then do You get that living water?" (4:11). She knew from experience how bad things could get if a woman belittled the fragile ego of a prideful man. To bring the man down to earth a bit, yet not offend him too much, she enlisted the common spiritual heritage that surrounded them and remarked: "You are not greater than our father Jacob, are You, who gave us the well, and drank of it himself?" (v. 12). She is trying to ground the conversation and politely tell this stranger that he is not God's gift to women. I'm confident she wanted this conversation to be over quickly and peaceably. She didn't want to feed the man's ego, but she also didn't want to shatter it either. Maybe she would have been bolder if anyone else had been around, but the safety of a crowd was not on her side. She didn't know what kind of a lunatic he was. She just wanted to get what she came for and leave. So she respectfully continued to play along but kept bringing the conversation back to earth.

Jesus, who was not at all disturbed by her obvious discomfort with the conversation, or for the potential misunderstanding she might be operating under, replied, "Everyone who drinks of this water will thirst again; but whoever drinks of the water that I will give him shall never thirst; but the water that I will give him will become in him a well of water springing up to eternal life" (vv. 13–14).

Probably wearing a sarcastic smile, the woman likely sighed or released a small grunt as she lifted the heavy, water-filled pot from the deep shaft. Playing along with the man's foolishness, she said, "Sir, give me this water, so I will not be thirsty nor come all the way here to draw" (v. 15).

She was not serious and likely not even amused, but Jesus was very serious. Jesus told her to get her husband and come back, and he would give her the eternally refreshing water of life. Sometimes in life you have no idea how significant something is that you are asking for. We often are in moments that we think have no importance at all, but actually they will change everything for us. This woman was blindly in such a moment.

The woman probably thought he was fishing to see if she was available or not. Much like the desperate pick-up artist who notices the lack of a wedding ring and then asks, "So what's your boyfriend think about . . . ," she thought he was hoping she was unattached and available. Either way, she had no intention of hiking back up the hill, finding someone, and bringing him all the way back down to meet this strange Jew who lacked any social awareness. Little did she know that in a few minutes she would be doing just that, but with a whole lot more than one man.

In another attempt to shrug him off, she gave him a half truth that allowed her to not have to actually respond to his request. She stated matter-of-factly, "I have no husband" (v. 17).

It was at this moment the entire tone of the conversation changed dramatically. The woman probably thought this was just one more time she would have to deal with a man being a man. She had no idea this conversation was a whole different kind of pick-up line.

Jesus responded in a matter-of-fact manner as well: "You have correctly said, 'I have no husband'; for you have had five husbands, and the one whom you now have is not your husband; this you have said truly" (vv. 17–18).

The biblical text doesn't say this, but you have to imagine there was a long pause after that seemingly casual remark. Now the air suddenly became heavy. All breath was gone from her lungs. Adrenalin shot through her body, raising every hair on its tip. All her senses suddenly became alert. Everything she thought this conversation was about had been incorrect. This man was not at all what she thought. In fact, this casual conversation was not as spontaneous as she thought. A sense of destiny suddenly cast its shadow on this presumably casual moment.

All kinds of scary thoughts shot through her mind at the same time. *How does he know who I am? Has he been stalking me? No, that wouldn't be possible in our village. Did he talk with someone? No, that's not likely either. Did I say something about this to him? No, I didn't. Have we met before? No, I'd remember that! How does he know me? What is going on here? What sort of magic is this? Is it possible that he is a prophet? Is God telling him about me? Why? To what end? What importance can I possibly have to God or this prophet? If he's a prophet, maybe I can find some answers about other things . . .*

After a poignant pause full of silence and lots of rapid-fire thoughts, the woman finally asked a question that had plagued her and her people for a long time. It is the most important spiritual question she could think of, and fortunately it would take the focus of their conversation off her shameful past. She asked, "Sir, I perceive that You are a prophet. Our fathers worshiped in this mountain, and you people say that in Jerusalem is the place where men ought to worship" (vv. 19–20).

"Woman," Jesus replied, "believe Me, an hour is coming when neither in this mountain nor in Jerusalem will you worship the Father" (v. 21). In one sentence Jesus disintegrated centuries of theological debate. In a sense, both sides were insufficient for the one true God.

But he is not saying that both sides are wrong, because that wouldn't be right either, and that is what she was asking, so he goes further and answers her question: "You worship what you do not know; we worship what we know, for salvation is from the Jews" (v. 22). There, he settled the debate—you're wrong, we're right, but that is not what is important. External places of worship are not what are actually important at all. The real significance was not where you are and how you practice religious rituals. The most important thing, the one and only thing that matters, was what was inside of you! Holy practices, holy days, and holy sites are not important; only one thing is truly important. God is seeking for you to be his worshiper from the heart, in spirit and in truth. True spirituality is a one-thing spirituality.

Jesus said, "But an hour is coming, and now is, when the true worshipers will worship the Father in spirit and truth; for such people the Father seeks to be His worshipers. God is spirit, and those who worship Him must worship in spirit and truth" (vv.

23–24). It's not important where you go to seek God, because God has been seeking you. In fact, he has sought you here, at the noon hour, at this old well, at this very moment.

This conversation gets more terrifying by the second. If the woman felt fearful before, now she was suddenly aware of the true significance of this holy moment. There was silence, and even in her own mind, I imagine the number of thoughts diminished to one: *Is this possible? Is this happening?*

After the silence, she finally ventured a slow, broken statement seeking confirmation of what she was thinking: "I know that Messiah is coming (He who is called Christ); when that One comes, He will declare all things to us" (v. 25). I imagine the tone at the end of her sentence rose in inquiry as if a question, but she couldn't bring herself to actually ask it. For some reason it just felt safer to make a theological statement. It's too much to actually ask straight out.

Then Jesus declared with a gleam in his eye and confidence in his words, "I who speak to you am He" (v. 26).

Whoa. This *was* happening!

At that moment the disciples returned and felt the awkwardness of the situation they stumbled into. Seeing their rabbi speak to a woman, a Samaritan woman, in public was beyond their imagination.

> The Rabbinic precept ran: "Let no one talk with a woman in the street, no, not with his own wife." The Rabbis so despised women and so thought them incapable of receiving any real teaching that they said: "Better that the words of the law should be burned than delivered to women." They had a saying: "Each time that a man prolongs converse with a woman he causes evil to himself, and desists from the law, and in the end inherits

Gehinnom." By Rabbinic standards, Jesus could hardly have done a more shatteringly unconventional thing than to talk to this woman. Here is Jesus taking the barriers down.[1]

The disciples were observant enough to keep their mouths shut and not disrupt the conversation, even though they were all wondering why Jesus was talking to this woman and what they were talking about. They just observed in silence.

The woman saw an opportunity to finally leave the conversation, but not for the same reason as before. In fact, she left her water pot behind and rushed to the village to tell everyone what had just happened to her. Leaving her water pot shows us that she had every intention of returning and wanted to make haste up to the village and tell everyone about this man she met. She didn't leave to get away but to bring others to share what she had discovered. She said to her fellow villagers, "Come, see a man who told me all the things that I have done; this is not the Christ, is it?" (v. 29).

Meanwhile, at the well, the disciples encouraged Jesus to eat something, but he was feeling quite satisfied with his rich encounter. Jesus, savoring the Spirit in such a holy moment, simply said, "I have food to eat that you do not know about" (v. 32). This confused the disciples a bit, as you can imagine, so he explained, "My food is to do the will of Him who sent Me and to accomplish His work" (v. 34). That is one-thing spirituality, isn't it? There is a deep contentedness that is only possible when we are in tune with the Spirit and doing His will. It satisfies our whole being in a way nothing else can.

While they were still digesting that statement, Jesus took the conversation a step further. He said, "Do you not say, 'There are yet four months, and then comes the harvest'? Behold, I say to you, lift up your eyes and look on the fields, that they are white for harvest" (v. 35).

The traditional garment of Samaritans was white. I believe at this moment a crowd of Samaritan villagers descended the hill toward the well to see the man the woman told them about. Jesus pointed to them, all dressed in white, and quoted a familiar Jewish proverb about waiting four months for a harvest to his disciples. He said, "Look! There it is! White and ready in a place you never expected and at a time you least expected."

The villagers asked Jesus and his disciples to stay, and they did for two days, and many came to believe in him. This woman who was alone and ostracized from her village was used to bring them to Christ. Everyone in town knew her, and six of the men knew her in the biblical sense of the word. Women didn't like her; men didn't respect her. Because of the lust of men and her own weaknesses, she was living a life well below all her hopes and dreams as a young girl. She was at the well in the heat of the afternoon because she didn't feel welcome with the other women of the village when they usually drew water. Jesus used the unusable. He opened the eyes of the disciples to see a ripe harvest in a place no one expected, using a person no one would listen to. Brant Hansen brilliantly described this moment in a tweet recently:

I love how subversively wonderful Jesus is. His first missionary? A woman (!) with a bad sexual reputation (!!) Who held wrong doctrinal beliefs!!![2]

A one-of-a-kind conversation with Jesus, and she became the source of spiritual awakening for this town that once hated her. Jesus gave her the living water that changed everything. She would probably still go to the well every day, but never without thinking about that one day. And she would never thirst again. After a lifetime of searching for love in all the wrong places, Jesus satisfied the longing of her soul. What her religion and six different men failed to do, Jesus did.

THE WOMAN CAUGHT IN ADULTERY

In a volatile moment with a mob on the verge of violence, Jesus stepped to the center and drew the attention of the crowd away from a half-dressed woman who had been caught in a shameful moment and dragged into public view as a spectacle. Without tear gas, helmets, Plexiglas shields, billy clubs, or fire hoses, Jesus dispersed the mob with only a few gestures and a single sentence. With little time to think, his wisdom, justice, and love were put to the test in extreme fashion.

Drawing all attention to himself and away from the poor woman, he bent down and doodled something in the dirt. Some speculate he wrote down the sins of each one there without assigning them to the guilty parties—sort of an implied and incomplete game of connect-the-dots.

Though we don't know what Jesus wrote, we do know that all eyes and ears were suddenly on him rather than on the woman. His answer to their demand for justice was a single sentence: "He who is without sin among you, let him be the first to throw a stone at her" (John 8:7). Just like that, he dispersed the crowd and subdued the violence. He did this to bring a single lost lamb into the safety of the fold and to hold up a mirror to the would-be wolves so they could see their own sheepishness.

Everyone walked away with something to think about in their own spiritual health and formation. Each person felt a bit exposed, but not wanting to be judged by their own standard of justice. The truth is, if not for the work of our great Shepherd, we're all walking targets for the stones of judgment.

Even for the woman caught in the act of adultery, Jesus spoke loving words of truth to bring about healing and restoration. As he often did, he started with a question: "Did no one condemn you?" (v. 10).

Clinging desperately to whatever she had to cover her nakedness, the woman answered in tears, probably gasping for air amid sobs of fear, shame, and grief: "No one, Lord" (v. 11).

Of course, the answer was sort of obvious. Everyone had left. A random scattering of sharp stones in the dust were the most articulate witnesses in this mock trial. So why did Jesus ask the question? He always asked questions because it drew out confessions from people. Confession results in healing, and Jesus was always about healing people in every way possible. Jesus wanted her to know she had come very close to being executed, but that she was not alone in her sin. Her guilt was real, though it was not hers alone.

He then said, "I do not condemn you, either" (v. 11).

Here was someone who could have thrown the first stone, but he chose not to. Instead, he said, "Go. From now on sin no more" (v. 11). In other words, "The rocks of judgment and condemnation may not have hit you, but you've certainly hit rock bottom. Now is the time to turn your life around. Now is your second chance. Don't blow it. From this point on, you are to be different."

Always looking to strengthen people and draw out what is needed for their healing and growth, Jesus, the Shepherd, touched the hearts of all who were there. He cared about the ones with the stones as well as the one who was the target. He was able to defuse the problem without taking sides—by taking both sides! He didn't attack one or the other.

Jesus is the great Shepherd (1 Peter 2:25; 5:4). He calls to the sheep, and they hear his voice and follow him. He goes after the lost sheep and brings them lovingly back into the fold. He sees value in those who are deemed less valuable by others, and he draws out their value for others to see. He even loved his enemies and prayed for those who persecuted him. In the end, he laid down his life for his sheep. Jesus is the ultimate Shepherd, the example to us all.

We are left with some obvious questions at the end of this story. Where was the man who was caught in the act of adultery? Why was it that the world always seems to hold women more responsible for sexuality than men, when men drive the sexually immoral business more than women? This is unjust and evil. Would Jesus have said and done the same if a man had been brought before him? I believe so, but we will never know for certain.

Again we see a story where a woman in crisis, because of a man in her life, came into contact with Jesus and was set free. We do not know what happened after this story. I imagine her life among neighbors, friends, and family hit some rough spots. We do not know if this changed her life. We don't know the condition of her spiritual life. What we do know is that her life was about to be lost because of a relationship with a man who was suddenly and conveniently gone. We also know that this woman was exposed and vulnerable and about to be executed. And we know that her life was spared by Jesus, our Savior and hers.

The good news of Jesus is for everyone. It is the same news for everyone. God shows no partiality (Gal. 2:6). Every person who comes to Christ and chooses to follow him receives the same gift of salvation. There is no one who receives more salvation than another. All of us in Christ are coheirs with him and with one another.

Paul summarized this idea by saying:

> So in Christ Jesus you are all children of God through faith, for all of you who were baptized into Christ have clothed yourselves with Christ. There is neither Jew nor Gentile, neither slave nor free, nor is there male and female, for you are all one in Christ Jesus. If you belong to Christ, then you are Abraham's seed, and heirs according to the promise. (Gal. 3:26–29 NIV)

As one takes into account the teaching of the new covenant and the whole of what we all receive for following Christ, the natural result is equality. We simply cannot treat a son or daughter of the King of kings in any way inferior to others. There is a lift for anyone who comes to Christ that sets them free, empowers them with a holy presence, and grants them an immediate purpose that is bigger than their own life.

Rachel Held Evans posted this thought online that deserves mentioning:

> Jesus did theology among the outliers—the poor, the sick, the marginalized, women, Samaritans, fishermen—and he was rejected by the religious elite. "I praise you, Father, Lord of heaven and earth," Jesus proclaimed, "because you have hidden these things from the wise and learned, and revealed them to little children." Theology is for everyone. And if theology doesn't make sense among the very people Jesus centered his ministry around, then it doesn't make sense. If it's not good news for the poor, it's not good news. If it's not good news for the hungry,

it's not good news. If it's not good news for the weak, it's not good news. If it's not good news for the oppressed, the forgotten, the hurting, the lonely, the people who hunger and thirst for righteousness, the spiritually and physically sick, then it's not good news. The gospel isn't the gospel when it belongs to the powerful to dispense, explain, and exclude as they see fit.[3]

Whatever status in life you come from, when you step into Christ, you are changed even if your status is not. There is a redemptive lift that affects people and eventually culture and society as a whole. This is the good news that we believe, accept, and proclaim—at least it should be. The world is ready for it.

I cannot help but think that we can step in and help women more often the way Jesus did. We would not need to have the power to heal or revelation of each person's sin to do so; we simply need to be an advocate for women. Even if they are responsible in part for the sin in their lives, we can speak up for them and, like Jesus, give them the chance to set their lives on a better path.

I would love if followers of Christ lived up to the good news they proclaim to believe in. We have plentiful opportunities to become good news to women in this world who have received so much abuse from men. Perhaps if we were good news, people would be more inclined to listen to the good news we have been given.

Jesus was a revolutionary who brought lasting change to the way women are perceived in society. The first words of the New Testament are a genealogy of Jesus. One would think that a genealogy is not that interesting to start with and not a way to empower women, but in this case you would be wrong.

It was unheard of to include a woman in a genealogy, no matter how interesting or historic she might have been. But in Jesus' genealogy not one woman but four are mentioned. What is even more fascinating is that the women mentioned are not pillars of character and utmost reputation in a Jewish culture. Tamar pretended to be a prostitute (can you actually sell sex and still be pretending?) to sleep with her father-in-law to prove a point. Ruth was a Moabite. Bathsheba was an adulteress and perhaps complicit in the murder of her first husband. Mary was an unwed teenage mother. What does this tell us? It shows us that Jesus loves women as much as men. It also tells us that women who sin are no worse than men who sin. His coming brought an empowerment to the status of women, even if it takes many centuries for this to take root in society. Societies built on the gospel of Jesus empower women's rights far more than those built on any other religious message. Like the abolitionist movement, the suffragette movement was advanced by Quakers and other followers of Christ set free by the gospel.

In a world where men get away with sin and women get punished for the same, Jesus leveled the field of justice with his grace and mercy freely bestowed on all equally. We may not get to meet the man caught in adultery in the Bible, but he is known by God and his justice and his mercy are doled out equally. There is a redemptive lift the gospel brings to people in a society where the good news of Jesus is found.

Chapter 10

JESUS TAKES ON WORSHIP

Men never do evil so completely cheerfully as
when they do it from religious conviction.
—BLAISE PASCAL

With or without religion, good people can behave
well and bad people can do evil; but for good
people to do evil—that takes religion.
—STEVEN WEINBERG

I asked a conservative Christian audience to raise their hands if they would like to have the reputation of Jesus in this world. All hands raised immediately and enthusiastically. I then informed them that Jesus had a reputation of being an alcoholic who welcomed intimate physical affection from prostitutes (Luke 7:31–50). I then asked, "So how's that going for you?"

My friend Alan Hirsch said, "If you're not known as a friend of sinners and offending Pharisees, you're not being conformed to the image of Jesus."[1] The scary thing to ask is, What are you being conformed to, if not Jesus? Perhaps that is not so hard to answer.

The Pharisees, in contrast to Jesus, had a reputation for being extremely committed to the Scriptures and a strong moral character. They were intelligent, well spoken, unsoiled by worldly pleasures, and best known for their spiritual beliefs and sacrifices. They stood up against what was seen as evil with strong convictions and statements of uncompromising passion for God.

Though we'd never admit it, given the choice, I think we would choose the reputation of the Pharisees more than Jesus. Our actions betray that. What's worse is that we can easily be convinced that such a choice is actually the more spiritual option. Believe it or not, we can easily justify that a more Christian reputation is to be like the Pharisees rather than Christ, even though the word *Christian* means to be "little Christs." We are deceived into thinking that taking an outspoken moral stand against something is the more spiritual path than engaging immoral people with love and personal identification. Would we be willing to actually risk our pharisaical reputation in this world to truly identify with broken people and shake the foundations of the established religious institution as Jesus did?

Paul clearly made a distinction in Galatians between those who invest in human-generated spirituality and those who walk by grace. Those who live for the approval of men as their desired spiritual makeup would compromise to do so and, in the end, would not please God, or very many people for that matter. Those who walk by the Spirit do not cater to the whims and opinions of others. The result is persecution. Paul said, "If I still preach circumcision, why am I still persecuted? Then the stumbling block of the cross has been abolished" (Gal. 5:11). The true gospel has a price, and it leads to persecution not popularity.

Our true gospel-generated spirituality is not subject to the opinions of others. As Paul said, "For am I now seeking the favor of men, or of God? Or am I striving to please men? If I were still trying to please men, I would not be a bond-servant of Christ" (Gal. 1:10).

In this chapter I will demonstrate how Christ responded to the religious people around him in contrast to today's typical Christian reactivity. After that, I will contrast how the worship system of the day responded to Christ's ministry versus our own. First, however, I want to show how our attempt to Christianize the world is a complete failure.

DO WE WANT A CHRISTIANIZED SHARIA LAW?

When we hear stories about Muslims wishing to establish Sharia law over an area, it offends us as Christians. How can they force people to believe in something and to conform their behavior to suit a religion? But I believe we have done just that. We have tried to enforce on our nation a type of Christianized Sharia law.

We fight one moral battle after another trying to enforce our belief system and worldview on others—legally, of course. We used to have laws prohibiting the sale of alcohol. We used to make businesses close on Sundays. We once had strict anti-gambling laws (now our states are making billions on the backs of poor people with lotteries). We once had very strict laws for two people to get a divorce. We even had a say in people's bedrooms with sodomy laws prohibiting homosexuality. We once could see the residue of our Christian faith in a myriad of laws. How is that really any different than Sharia law? In fact, much of the laws cross over. Sharia law also prevents divorce, sodomy, the sale of alcohol, and closes businesses on Saturdays.

These laws were enacted because Christians made up the majority of the population and so the laws made sense. Those days have long gone. Those laws succumbed to the true spiritual-ism of our country: capitalism.

Here are a few examples of the moral and spiritual battles we wage fighting for a residue of the faith once inherent in our population but is no longer. I hope that we can begin to see that fighting over these things gets us nowhere.

- Every public school used to open with prayer each day. Today we fight to have prayer in the public schools, whether it is in a convocation or a private prayer meeting on campus during school hours. Of course, this isn't bad, but why do we think it is justified to legally impose such rules on a secular government? Really, how is that different from the Muslim call to prayer several times a day? You do not need laws to pray, and no law can stop me from praying.

- We fight to allow a plaque listing the Ten Commandments on our courthouses. Is that really necessary? Why should our local or federal courts have to display our religious foundation? The law is written on our hearts, and I, for one, would rather they see it in my words and deeds than have to read it on a plaque.

- We have fights to keep "under God" in the Pledge of Allegiance. Why? It's not like making people say it makes it any more true. We fight these things as if losing would mean our faith has lost the war. If that is the case, then our faith lost the war a long time ago. If having Christian laws imposed on non-Christians is how we establish our influence on society, we are fighting the wrong war.

- Marriage laws are an interesting debate topic now. This is fascinating because churches and clergy are a big part of marriage in our culture, so we should have a say in what marriage is, right? For a long time we have been saying, "By the authority vested in me by the state of—, I now pronounce you husband and wife." To be honest, I wonder why the church has such a role in marriage. Nowhere in the Bible does it say that churches are where weddings are done and clergy are supposed to officiate them. This tradition is from Roman Catholic dogma and a society that is long gone. It is actually the government that gives that authority to us, not the Bible. If the government wants to take back that authority, can we appeal to a higher source? Should we?

In the Bible we can certainly find God's opinion about marriage and we do not have to go very far. "For this reason a man shall leave his father and his mother, and be joined to his wife; and they shall become one flesh" (Gen. 2:24). I believe that marriage is between a man and a woman and that is the way God designed it. This makes sense biblically, biologically, and socially.

This informs my worldview, and in a democratic nation I will vote with these things in mind when given a choice. In a free democratic nation, I have a voice and a vote, and to that extent I will try to make a difference. That is my legal right and it is also yours; at least for now. But if we spend all our influence this way, do we not lose the better influence of the gospel in the process? When we are only known as standing against certain morals, and our message is not love, we are losing more than we could ever gain.

Because my nation decided to redefine marriage so that two men or two women can legally be wed, do I have any authority to tell them otherwise if they reject my view of the Bible? If I appeal to the Bible, and they do not follow its tenets, should I force them to? Of course not. Enforced morality or spirituality has never been the way of Jesus. Yet we have attempted as much many times and likely will again. One can argue that the very reason we have lost so much true influence is because we have only fought for legal moral enforcement. Shouldn't I wish the best for all people and not for their misfortune?

A PERSECUTED CHURCH?

So if I say, as a pastor, that I will not perform any same-sex weddings, that is certainly my prerogative, just as two people of the same sex now have the prerogative to get married in our society. At least that is so for now. What if the government determines that my choosing not to perform same-sex marriages is a hateful exclusion and that I must perform same-sex weddings or allow them on my church properties? Am I willing to leave everything on that battle front when there is not a shred of biblical support for clergy's performing weddings or churches being wedding sites or even churches having properties? I personally will not die for that cause. If two people want to get married, and the Supreme Court says they can, who am I to tell them they can't? Like everyone else, they will give an account of their choices to God, not to me. I am not judging them. I actually think it is not my business if two men or two women want to get married and live their lives together, and I personally do not want to be known as someone who is against such things. I would much rather give up the privilege of officiating weddings than fight this fight. It amazes me how invested the church is in marrying people and not in making disciples. The Bible clearly tells us to do one, and nowhere does it give us the other task.

Some may say that we have already lost so much in our society that we need to fight for everything we can. By that logic I would say the war was lost long ago. The very reason we have such battles now is because our society has left the mores of Christian faith long ago, and making them comply with our moralities now is useless. We cannot and should not try to climb our way back into the 1950s. Instead, we should approach this generation with a vital gospel, as missionaries to a world that is not our home, rather than beat them up with legislated morality. We should see ourselves as missionaries in a foreign field that is not Christian. Until we do, our expectations, strategies, and purposes will be all messed up. Our mission is not to set up a more Christian nation but to bring the rule and reign of Jesus to those who are lost and dying. Unfortunately, too often we sacrifice the later on the altar of the former. A missionary reaching out to a nation that practices polygamy would be more effective sharing the gospel and changing lives than marriage laws. In fact, marriage laws may eventually change because more lives are changed. Why can't we see our own position in this country the same way?

Once our moral and spiritual battles in this country were about enforcing a Christian moralism in our society; today, we are actually trying to keep secularism from making our beliefs illegal. We have lost the moral high ground, and as a result, we are going to be punished under the law for not being in line with a secular, politically correct morality. We must come to the recognition that we are closer to being persecuted for our faith than getting the world to conform to our moral codes.

As the prophet Amos said, "I am not a prophet, nor am I the son of a prophet" (7:14), but for the sake of discussion, let me map out a few steps that would permanently alter church as we know it. In fact, it wouldn't take much persecution to dismantle most churches, just a few legal changes that are already likely being considered.

If the following benefits were revoked, many churches would close: tax deductions for contributions and tax-exempt status for churches and parsonage allowances. I say this because the way we do church is so expensive that we rely on these special privileges to survive. This is especially true in a struggling economy, where the government is looking for ways to reduce its deficits and increase revenue to provide more services for its constituents—services that churches no longer supply to their communities.

If you are a church leader, I suggest you ask yourself how your church would survive if these three tax benefits were revoked. That is far better than to simply write off what I am saying by telling yourself this could never happen. Crunch the numbers. Do the math. It will be scary but may lead to some good, sound steps to be better prepared.

Few ordinary citizens know about this special perk that pastors get, called the parsonage allowance. I have enjoyed this benefit, and to be honest, I don't even know why it is afforded to me. All money spent on housing (rent, mortgage, utilities, furniture, home improvements, repairs, upkeep, and supplies) can be taken off the salary of a paid church leader even up to the entire amount they are paid in salary. I feel like I am betraying our special club for even writing about it publicly, like I might jinx it. Add to that the fact that church leaders are able to opt out of Social Security, and you can easily see how pastors are able to get by on much less than the rest. This sounds like a Michael Moore movie waiting to happen.

A pastor being paid at a lower-middle-class economic level can live at a mid- to high–middle-class standard because of these perks. And churches can hire more staff because of these advantages. If you don't think churches rely on this, your head is in the sand.

With the parsonage allowance, a pastor's support can double, allowing a church to maintain a professional staff twice the size it can actually afford. Nevertheless, smaller churches are already unable to afford their pastors. Most churches have far more ministry than they have leaders. The more a church relies upon a professional staff, the more vulnerable it is in this way.

If the special perk of the parsonage allowance were taken away, we would see an immediate hardship on churches struggling to keep their staff employed. The number of unemployed pastors is already high, but this would flood the market with unemployable church leaders whose only skill is exegeting Greek and Hebrew and preaching sermons. Once this happens, seminaries would probably go out of business as quickly as smaller churches. No one would be able to afford to pursue a professional degree that doesn't ultimately lead to employment.

If churches cannot afford their pastors, they would likely also not support their missionaries. Mission agencies would be just as vulnerable, if not more so. Parachurch organizations too. Removal of this one benefit could be all it takes, but there are other legal vulnerabilities as well.

What would happen if our churches were forced to pay property taxes? This would push most churches over the edge, at least in their current form, especially if the perks mentioned above were also removed.

Most cities are already openly hostile to churches and are trying to prevent them from acquiring property, because there is no

income from these organizations. When city officials try to understand the benefit to the community these organizations provide
(from their perspective), they usually come up with only two things:
marrying and burying. The payoff isn't worth it. In many cases, the
local Denny's restaurant does more for the community than the
local church. At least Denny's provides jobs, meals, and pays taxes
for public services and city infrastructure. The typical church doesn't
do any of that. I cannot imagine the city of Houston isn't glaring
at Lakewood Church's $32 million annual income and wondering
what the property taxes should be.[2] The Houston Rockets used the
same facility more often during the week and paid their fair share of
taxes and gave the city a better show and two championships to celebrate. I'm sorry if this sounds offensive to Christian leaders, but I
want you to see that this is how the world views our special perks. A
scary question for most churchgoers: would your community even
notice if your church disappeared? I used to think that question was
harsh because the answer would be no, but now I fear it is even more
harsh because the answer is, "Yes, the community would notice." In
many cases the answer would be yes because there would actually
be more benefit to the community after the church closed and a
tax-paying business took its place.

A third law that could change is denying people the option to
write off their contributions to churches. If this changed, I am sure
that many churches would see their annual income drop severely.
I would like to think it isn't so, but why else is it that we count
on larger gifts at the end of the year? It's because we know people
are looking for tax breaks. Granted, this is likely the last perk to
be removed, because so many other nonprofits benefit from this.
Perhaps this could be engineered in specific examples for punitive
reasons.

What could possibly cause the government to take these privileges away? Besides the government's current multitrillion-dollar deficit and desire to raise revenues, the government has an increasingly hostile stance toward right-wing fundamentalists in our nation who benefit from all these laws. There are some tangible reasons that may lead to these changes. If the church is labeled as hateful, then the government would feel obligated to punish it in an attempt to correct inappropriate behavior. The government's first punitive move is always economic sanctions. This would not be the first time our government has used tax laws to leverage conformity.

Now that the laws are passed that allow for gay marriage, soon laws will be passed that require organizations not to discriminate in hiring practices based upon gender or sexual preference; many churches will be found on the wrong side of these laws. Some churches will fall in line and avoid penalties, but others will not, and they will face increasingly stiffer punitive restrictions. Passing such laws is not the persecution that will come, but merely the initial movements to set us up for it. These small changes alone may be enough to close a majority of the churches in America.

We already have earned a reputation of being intolerant in our society. Evangelical and fundamental expressions of Christianity are too closely tied to the Tea Party and Republican agendas, and they have consistently decried those who have entitlements. This will set us up for public mockery—something we should be used to by now. When these laws take our own entitlements away and we are found complaining louder than all others, our reputation as hypocrites will be confirmed in the eyes of the world and will only expedite passage of these laws.

It is ironic that we cling so tightly to our own tax entitlements when Jesus actually did the opposite. Once, he actually paid a tax he was exempt from so as not to offend people (Matt. 17:24–27). We do not see many followers of Christ following that example.

This damage to our reputation (some earned and some not), and subsequent increases in financial penalties, combined with a weak economy, will greatly reduce the local churches' income, and many (if not most) will not survive. It's a simple scenario, and as you can see, it is not only possible, but there is movement to already enact some of these measures. Is your church getting ready?

Our vulnerability is quite obvious. These three areas of dependence will kill us. What is interesting is that none of them are truly biblical, and yet they are central in importance to the way church is done in our society. In fact, it is how we are even identified as a church by our own culture and society. That is the saddest part to me. Where does the Bible say that pastors or churches perform weddings and funerals? It doesn't. There is not a single church building in all of the New Testament. Jesus didn't perform the wedding in Cana; he was just the beverage supplier. Why do we risk our character, reputation, and influence fighting for these things that are not even found in our Bible? The bigger question is, Why do we neglect so easily the things that are in the Bible, the care for the poor, orphans, and widows?

Would the church survive these legal changes? Some would; many would not. Those that would survive will find they must become simpler, more organic, and even underground. We must decrease our dependence on buildings, budgets, and big shots. We must also respond to our society with love rather than with lobbying for self-interested legislature.

It may be a shock to us that the government is against us, but it shouldn't be so. We are unique in history to be part of a nation where freedom of religion is a basic right and where our government has actually been in favor of our faith. We have had almost 240-plus years of no government persecution for our faith. That may cause us to settle into a form of entitlement, but should we? I suspect we should prepare ourselves to experience what Christians throughout time have coped with: persecution.

Jesus told us in advance that the world hated him and it would hate us (John 15:18–25). If it doesn't hate us, we should ask ourselves why. All who desire to live godly in Christ will be persecuted (2 Tim. 3:12). He told us that we are blessed when we are persecuted (Matt. 5:10–12). We should not only expect persecution, we should see it as an opportunity. Whenever the church is persecuted it thrives. Many have been praying for years for revival. Will we complain when God answers our prayers?

My experience is that government is not the sole culprit of persecution. It is often the reigning and previous religious system that leads the charge against the church. Usually, the two work together. There is good reason for this. The raising of a people who are truly sold out to Christ is threatening to the institutions of power in the world, whether religious or governmental. That is as much the case today as ever, and persecution of Christ followers is increasing all over the world today. Friendly fire isn't friendly, but it is common where the kingdom is advancing.

Jesus himself was at the receiving end of persecution from both the Jewish religious leaders and the Roman government. In fact, what strange bedfellows hatred for a spiritual person creates. The Jews hated the Romans with a passion, yet they called on the emperor as the only king to get Jesus crucified. Pilate asked them why they would want the King of the Jews crucified. The reply from the religious leaders was astonishing. The chief priests answered,

"We have no king but Caesar" (John 19:15). Their hatred of Christ trumped their hatred for Rome.

In the rest of this chapter, we will see how Jesus was a rebel against the worship system of his day. We will see how he revolted against the religious doctrines and practices, the religious leaders behind them, and even against the worship center and system itself.

JESUS REVOLTED AGAINST RELIGIOUS DOCTRINES AND PRACTICES

Jesus was a real threat to the religious leaders of his day. He fulfilled perfectly every biblical command of the Old Testament without fail (Matt. 5:17–20). The unbiblical commands that came from the traditions of men, however, he seemed to go out of his way to break publicly.

Jesus rejected any laws made by men, and for good reason. God is the lawgiver, and when men establish laws as God's, they are putting themselves in the position of deity. The religious leaders of the time had centuries of traditions that became laws. At first the traditions were meant as a protective hedge to keep people from violating God's law, but eventually those hedges became walls and then laws. Jesus went out of his way to demonstrate that those traditional laws had no authority. He broke the human laws of the Sabbath, dietary restrictions, temple worship, and laws of cleanliness.

It was not just his actions that rattled the religious leaders, but he actually challenged their doctrines. He took their twisted laws and nullified them and demanded a higher level (Matt. 5:21–48). In fact, the Sermon on the Mount is an indictment of the Pharisees from start to finish (Matt. 5–7).

The religious leaders questioned him about the lack of obedience to their doctrines (Mark 7:1–7). His response was straightforward and cutting:

> Then some Pharisees and scribes came to Jesus from Jerusalem and said, "Why do Your disciples break the tradition of the elders? For they do not wash their hands when they eat bread." And He answered and said to them, "Why do you yourselves transgress the commandment of God for the sake of your tradition? For God said, 'Honor your father and mother,' and, 'He who speaks evil of father or mother is to be put to death.' But you say, 'Whoever says to his father or mother, "Whatever I have that would help you has been given to God," he is not to honor his father or his mother.' And by this you invalidated the word of God for the sake of your tradition. You hypocrites, rightly did Isaiah prophesy of you:
>
> > 'This people honors Me with their lips,
> > But their heart is far away from Me.
> > 'But in vain do they worship Me,
> > Teaching as doctrines the precepts of men.'"

After Jesus called the crowd to Him, He said to them, "Hear and understand. It is not what enters into the mouth that defiles the man, but what proceeds out of the mouth, this defiles the man."

Then the disciples came and said to Him, "Do You know that the Pharisees were offended when they heard this statement?" But He answered and said, "Every plant which My heavenly Father did not plant shall be uprooted. Let them alone; they are blind guides of the blind. And if a blind man guides a blind man, both will fall into a pit." (Matt. 15:1–14)

JESUS REVOLTED AGAINST THE RELIGIOUS LEADERS

Not only did he attack their doctrines, he went after the leaders themselves. Jesus was not shy about confronting the leaders of this illegitimate religious institution, because they were at the heart of the abuses. And he didn't hold back any punches. Sixteen times he used the word *hypocrite* to describe the religious leaders. It was one of his favorite descriptions of the leaders, which shows us much of how Jesus felt about them. This is not a congenial and diplomatic approach.

After he had dealt with the Pharisees who accused him of using demons to cast out demons (Luke 11:14–28), a Pharisee invited him to lunch (Luke 11:37). There are always some religious leaders who try to build bridges and mend relationships. Perhaps he wanted to correct Jesus in a more relational and less public setting. Perhaps he intended to prove something. Maybe he was setting Jesus up for an ambush; after all, we know that others were there as well, including experts in the law (Luke 11:45). We do not know why he asked Jesus to join him, but he did.

It was remarkable that the invitation was extended, and it was just as amazing that Jesus accepted the invitation. This was at a time when Jesus was increasing his bold confrontations with the religious leaders. In fact, he had just pronounced judgment on the generation: "This is a wicked generation. It asks for a sign, but none will be given it except the sign of Jonah" (Luke 11:29 NIV).

Jesus was not in a mellow, conciliatory mood. Nevertheless, when invited, he responded. Jesus took up the Pharisee's invitation, but he didn't soften his message at all.

The first thing the revolutionary did is actually something he *didn't* do. He didn't ceremonially wash his hands (Luke 11:38). This obviously shocked and offended his host. Jesus was not fooled by niceties that masked a false motive. But he still went to the Pharisee's home.

Washing your hands before eating is not a bad idea. We even have the proverb "Cleanliness is next to godliness." Cleanliness is a good thing, but to put it right next to godliness is a dangerous idea. Why? Because it doesn't take long before it is confused with godliness. Eventually man-made laws take precedence over those given to us by God. The Jews had a similar idea about cleanliness that eventually became holy writ and a law that carried the authority of Scripture commanding them to wash their hands in certain ways and at certain times. This is what Jesus didn't like: man-made laws that carried divine authority and compelled God's people to obey men rather than God. He actually accused the Pharisees of sitting in the seat of Moses, the lawgiver (Matt. 23:2). It is actually God who gives the law, and they were willing to view the world from his seat too.

When he saw indignation on the faces of the religious leaders, or perhaps even the smug look of some who had caught a mouse in a supposed trap, Jesus jumped right into the issue. He didn't mess around. Using the cleansing of hands as a launching pad, he accused the religious leaders of hypocrisy and called them foolish for doing so and believing it would work.

From that moment, still seated at the table, Jesus launched into a full pronouncement of judgment upon the religious leaders of the day, both the Pharisees and the legal experts. In rapid succession he let fly a chain of woes on them. He accused them of greed and withholding charity to those who have need (Luke 11:41). He accused them of neglecting justice (v. 42). He accused them of being religiously strict about minor things and missing the big picture (v. 42). He accused them of loving the admiration of people and the honors they received as leaders (v. 43). And he accused them of hypocrisy three times (vv. 39, 44, 46).

The lawyers were also offended and said as much, which was not a good idea. Jesus laid into them next. He accused them of weighing down people with burdens that no one could fulfill and that they themselves didn't even attempt to carry (Luke 11:46). He accused them of carrying the responsibility for killing the prophets that were sent to Israel even while they celebrated them later (vv. 47–48). He told them that they would prove him right by killing the prophets and apostles that God would send, and thereby carry the weight of guilt for all the generations up to this point (vv. 49–52).

He ended his accusations with a final woe to the legal experts: "Woe to you experts in the law, because you have taken away the key to knowledge. You yourselves have not entered, and you have hindered those who were entering" (Luke 11:52 NIV). In all the minutia of their doctrine, they ended up keeping God's people from any real understanding, and they themselves were also blind.

This was sort of a dampener to the brunch, as you can imagine. In fact, Jesus left right after these pronouncements and was followed by these leaders, all of them grilling him with questions, trying to catch him in a mistake. Needless to say, they failed miserably. They ended up having Jesus killed and thus verified the things Jesus said of them.

JESUS REVOLTED AGAINST THE WORSHIP CENTER AND SYSTEM

The temple was at the heart of the religion of his day. The temple of Christ's time, restored by Herod the Great, was an intimidating monument to the Jewish religion. Everything revolved around temple worship in the religion of Jesus' time. Jesus respected the Mosaic and Davidic laws, but not the goofed-up traditions and rules established by the ruling class of spiritual leaders. If he seemed bold in confronting the leaders before, his response to temple worship and religious business was outrageous and even bordering on violent.

Let's look at his response to the business practices that had invaded the household of God:

> Then they came to Jerusalem. And He entered the temple and began to drive out those who were buying and selling in the temple, and overturned the tables of the money changers and the seats of those who were selling doves; and He would not permit anyone to carry merchandise through the temple. And He began to teach and say to them, "Is it not written, 'My house shall be called a house of prayer for all the nations'? But you have made it a robbers' den." The chief priests and the scribes heard this, and began seeking how to destroy Him; for they were afraid of Him, for the whole crowd was astonished at His teaching. (Mark 11:15–18)

This was the last straw. It's one thing to correct their teaching and violate certain practices; it's another thing to attack their integrity as leaders. But to attack the heart of their religion, the temple itself, was not tolerable in any way.

Why were they so fearful and so murderously angry? Jesus' words were a double-edged indictment. God's people had substituted their true calling for a false identity. They had become distributors of religious goods and services and had abandoned their missional identity. They had become takers rather than givers. Instead of propagating the freedom of truth to all people without prejudice, they were focused on preserving the institution, financially and culturally, at all costs. They became a religious business that needed to be maintained rather than a missional spiritual family. Does that sound familiar?

Later, as they were walking around Jerusalem, the disciples were overwhelmed by the enormity and beauty of the temple. They called Jesus' attention to it, suspecting that he would affirm its importance and significance. He did not. Instead, he said, "Do you not see all these things? Truly I say to you, not one stone here will be left upon another, which will not be torn down" (Matt. 24:2).

At other times, Jesus referred to himself as a temple of God, and he predicted that he would be destroyed and raised up again three days later. Because the temple system was the heart of the religion of his day, it was this statement that the religious leaders used primarily as the false accusation in his mock trial.

We typically do the same thing as did the religious institution of Christ's day. The church today generally contains, conforms, and controls the believers in its care. Church leaders often neglect justice, make much of things that don't matter, and overlook the important things. Like the Pharisees and lawyers of Jesus' day, our leaders are often jockeying for positions of honor and come across as hypocrites. We enforce man-made rules to prevent people from sinning. Perhaps worst of all, we use doctrine to prevent people from really understanding God's true word. We also have turned worship into an enterprise; church has become a business that competes with other such businesses for a limited share of the market.

Jesus had great patience and showed much grace. God's patience is often called long-suffering because, frankly, his patience leads him to suffer long. I am simply stating that we need to stop seeing church through faulty lenses that ultimately corrupt our church practices and establish jaded views of success. Let's stop functioning like a business and start relating to one another like a body.

Facing a corrupt and self-benefiting system, Jesus addressed the problem forcefully by calling it out. He sharply contrasts what is in Scripture against what they were teaching and doing by saying, "Is it not written . . . ? But you have . . . ." If we wake up one day and find that our practices are not based on what is written in the Scriptures but are in fact opposing them, we need to abandon those practices in favor of the truth of God's Word, no matter how painful that may be. As I mentioned in the beginning, too often we resemble the Pharisees of Jesus' time more than we do Jesus.

Jesus struck hard at the religion of his day without pause or respect. He attacked their laws and principles, he trampled on their practices, he denounced the leaders who enforced them, and he vowed to tear down the building that housed them. Jesus was a true revolutionary, and he changed everything.

Lest you think that Jesus hated the self-righteous religious leaders of his day, I would remind you that he chose one of them to bear his gospel to the ends of the earth. In fact, that former Pharisee is the author of the letter to the Galatians from which much of this book draws its ideas. He would not stand for abuse of another person, but that doesn't mean he didn't love those who were abusive as much as those who were abused.

HOW PEOPLE RESPOND TO JESUS
AND TO US IS VERY DIFFERENT

We have already contrasted the reputations of Jesus and the Pharisees. But perhaps something even more telling was the response of the people to both. Broken, sinful, hurting people were enamored with Christ and sought him out. The highly religious conservative people hated Jesus and eventually arranged for his execution.

The true Jesus is not a safe, sterile, mild-mannered wimp conflicted by a mission and a passive kindness (which Hollywood typically portrays and Christians are comfortable believing in). He regularly said things that offended others. He never carried the party line. Jesus shocked his foes, his family, his friends, and his followers with equal doses.

In their book *Untamed,* Alan and Debra Hirsch wrote, "[Jesus'] was a wild holiness that calls to account all who refuse to deal with God, preferring instead to follow the lame dictates of a religion of ethical codes and pious rituals."[3]

The Hirsches went on to pose a revealing question and counter-question that opens our eyes to the tamed existence we have grown accustomed to: "What is it about the holiness of Jesus that caused 'sinners' to flock to him like a magnet and yet manages to seriously antagonize the religious people? This question begs yet another, even more confronting question: why does our more churchy form of holiness seem to get it the other way around?"

They went on to explain: "One of the greatest counterfeits for following the untamed Jesus comes from the substitution of morals and decency for Jesus' untamed kind of holiness. One of the standard attempts to stereotype, and therefore domesticate, Jesus is to make him into a moral Teacher, someone who taught us how to live decent, rule-based lives."

As C. H. Spurgeon commented: "Morality may keep you out of jail, but it will not keep you out of hell." The holiness of God is much more than a tamed and moral existence. Jesus was on a mission not to rescue those who were moral but those who were broken and imprisoned by evil. He was destined to reach into dark, sin-infested places to call out and redeem the beautiful image of God found in people who were enslaved by evil. He did not hang out in safe places. I would imagine that today you would be more likely to find Jesus in a gay bar than a church service. When he would go to a religious service, he may be likely to overturn the book tables and chase away the salespeople. He risked his reputation to be with the people who needed saving and knew they did. This is our Savior. His mission has not altered or changed in two thousand years, and he bids us to join him.

In today's climate we have gained the reputation of Pharisees. As such, we are beloved by religious conservative leaders (that is, as much as they can love anyone) and hated by the people who are broken, lost in sin, and marginalized in our culture.

It is my hope we can reverse this and launch a revolution of love much like Jesus did, because, frankly, our current path is not something I want to be part of anymore.

Conclusion

JESUS, THE REVOLUTIONARY

[I'm] so glad the Creator gave us more
than a book, a collection of rules, or lonely
"positive energy." He gave us a Person.

—BRANT HANSEN

Christians should be troublemakers, creators of uncertainty,
agents of a dimension incompatible with society.

—JACQUES ELLUL

Your vote is the only weapon you have in this war waged against godliness that is taking over our nation." I was driving with my radio tuned to Dr. James Dobson as he said those words. I almost missed my turn. Did he just say that? Is a vote the only weapon I have in the battle of good and evil, of darkness and light?

With all due respect to the founder of Focus on the Family, I have something stronger than my vote to change this world: I have the good news of Jesus. My vote can be stolen. I live in California where elections are often decided before a single vote is cast. In the last gubernatorial election, the incumbent didn't even campaign, and he won by a landslide. My vote in either direction would have had no impact whatsoever. Jesus, however, will never leave me or forsake me. He is always listening and caring. He is a lot more powerful than my vote. At best my vote could potentially help to change a law or a lawmaker, but Jesus can change a person from the inside out.

We can change our political affiliation and champion legislation and still be in the midst of darkness. I believe we actually are deceived into thinking one political party is more righteous than the other, or we can become more Christian as a nation by voting one way rather than the other. This is foolishness.

I believe we have let our allegiance to American democracy become more important to us than our role in God's kingdom. If the only hope we have against the encroaching spiritual darkness is our vote, then we're all doomed.

It is interesting that Jesus' life had so little to do with the government of his time. In fact, from what is written, he only encountered the governing powers at the very beginning of his life and at the very end. In both cases, the government intended to kill him. It finally succeeded because he was a threat to them. Herod the Great wanted Jesus dead as a small child simply because the newborn was called the king of the Jews. Since Herod was the king of the Jews, he felt threatened by this new arrival. The Romans' excuse for crucifying Jesus was that he claimed to be a king, and only the emperor could claim such a position.

It was prophesied of Jesus that the government would rest on his shoulders:

> For to us a child is born,
>   to us a son is given,
>   and the government will be on
>   his shoulders.

And he will be called
Wonderful Counselor, Mighty God,
Everlasting Father, Prince of Peace. (Isa. 9:6 NIV)

But Jesus really never addressed any government with counsel or correction. He didn't come to save governments but people. And neither are governments usually looking to Jesus for guidance.

Governments come and go, but Jesus and his kingdom are eternal and unshakable (Heb. 12:28). He didn't come to defend a nation or to overturn it. He came to establish a different kind of kingdom. Jesus never judged between people with complaints. He never proposed a law beyond "Love one another" (John 13:34). He never demanded a tax or declared war on a nation. So how is it that any government rests on his shoulders? He said to Pilate, "My kingdom is not of this world. If My kingdom were of this world, then My servants would be fighting so that I would not be handed over to the Jews; but as it is, My kingdom is not of this realm" (John 18:36).

Jesus' kingdom is not of this world but of a different world and a future reality. When the Pharisees and Herodians wanted to trap Jesus, they asked him about paying taxes. Jesus answered by identifying the currency as belonging to Caesar's rule and said, "Render to Caesar the things that are Caesar's; and to God the things that are God's" (Matt. 22:15–22). Jesus noticed the difference between the governments of men and his own kingdom. I truly wish we Christians would also recognize this difference and give our whole allegiance to the kingdom of God more than to our earthly nation. It appears that the currencies of the two entities are also entirely different, because what buys favor in one is of no value in the other.

Jesus' kingdom, however, is not a peaceful kingdom. On this side of Christ's second coming, the kingdom of God does not make violent strikes against others, but it receives violence often. Speaking of John the Baptist, who was beheaded, Jesus said, "From the days of John the Baptist until now the kingdom of heaven suffers violence, and violent men take it by force" (Matt. 11:12).

Pilate told Jesus at his trial that he had authority to release him or crucify him. Jesus replied, "You would have no authority over Me, unless it had been given you from above; for this reason he who delivered Me to you has the greater sin" (John 19:11). Jesus sees that governments exist only because God allows them to. This does not mean God is okay with everything governments do. Nothing escapes his notice or his eventual judgment.

I am fascinated by the fact that, at the end, after all the last days apocalyptic devastation, God will maintain the uniqueness of all the nations, and they will still have their own kings (Rev. 21:24–27). Granted, they will all be submitted to Christ as the King of kings. We see that the nations can bring glory to God and live in submission to Christ; they just usually don't.

Jesus lived in a time and place when many were waiting for a messianic leader to rise up and overthrow the Roman Empire. Among Jesus' band of disciples was a zealot who once lived for this. Nevertheless, Jesus would have none of that. His mission was much bigger than the Roman Empire. At one point these two ideas came into conflict. When the people saw one of Jesus' miracles, they said, "This is truly the Prophet who is to come into the world." Jesus perceived their intention of taking him by force to make him king, and he withdrew from the crowd (John 6:14–15).

In a sense the Roman Empire, which lasted in some form for more than fourteen hundred years, was not a big enough goal for

Jesus. His kingdom is eternal and ultimately will overcome every nation, every tribe, and every people (Rev. 5:9). His kingdom is not of this world, and his mission is bigger than this current world.

Jesus never endorsed a candidate or proposed legislation. He never attempted to change a government or any policies of any government. But he did change the world. Perhaps we settle for changing government policies and sacrifice changing the world in the process.

When he did encounter government, he addressed it as if he were an unbiased outsider, as if it were not his business. Even during his trial he seemed that way. Again, I wonder if we are so consumed with changing governments that we forfeit changing the world.

Should we refrain from trying to make a difference in our nation? There are examples of the kingdom of God having dramatic affect on society and legislation. The Quakers and the Methodists had a lot to do with changing things in England for the better in many important ways. In fact a prime factor in abolishing slavery was the influence of followers of Christ living out their own convictions as agents of the kingdom of God.

Quakers, who have a strong tenet of listening to God's voice, were a powerful force in both abolitionism and the suffragette movement. Many of the freedoms we experience in Western society can be traced to freedoms resulting from the gospel. I always find it more than a little curious when I see people attacking the faith with the freedom born from it. When revival hits, it changes a lot of things, laws and governments included, but those changes are a by-product of changed people.

During the Welsh revival, bars closed, crime evaporated, and police officers were laid off because so many lives changed. You couldn't accomplish that by trying to make those changes first. It is the gospel that changes lives, and when enough lives are changed, a law can be changed.

England abolished slavery because of the work of so many people who lived out the gospel. Revival had as much to do with it as legislation. It wasn't easy, but it came about over time because people themselves changed. In the States, however, it took a bloody civil war and decades of advocacy to enact change—and we are still at it. Trying to change a government (even a democratic one) from the outside, void of a change of heart by the gospel, lacks true effectiveness.

Some things were noticeably absent from Jesus' life:

1. As I said above, Jesus never endorsed candidates or proposed legislation. It is not as if the policies of the Roman and Jewish governments were so righteous he didn't need to address them. But he never attempted to change the government or any legislative policies.

2. He didn't take on the political or social issues of his day beyond caring for people in need. He never brought up any political plans or spoke against the government. If anything, he mentioned that the powers that existed to make policies were allowed to do so by the Father. And when people expected him to make political advancements, he retreated. His plan was to ignite a movement of changed people rather than to campaign for reformed government.

3. He didn't start an organization focused on a cause. After three to four years of living with a small band of followers, he left behind a family of disciples, not an organization.

He never set up a board or registered with a government agency. He asked permission or license from none. He resisted any sort of chain of command, organizational flow chart, or pyramid of authority (Mark 10:41–43).

4. He didn't intentionally raise donations, and when they were received unsolicited, he didn't care to govern them (John 12:6).

5. He didn't shame sinful people if they already felt shame. If they didn't, he still didn't overtly shame them but simply pointed out the consequences of their actions, unless they were religious leaders who were leading people astray. He humbled the proud and showed grace to the humbled.

Perhaps if we made the kingdom of God our primary allegiance, we would see more change among the kingdoms of the world today. If we followed Christ's example as laid out in the latter half of this book, we might see nations changed. We would be revolutionaries of a kingdom driven by love.

It is not new legislation that we need; it is a new creation.

SUMMARY

While I was writing this conclusion in a café, another customer asked me what I was writing. When I said it was about how true Christianity would change people rather than change laws, the woman's complexion went flush, her brows arched up, and her jaw dropped down. In a huff, she said, "Well those are the two topics I try to avoid most: religion and politics." With that she eagerly moved on.

Jesus is a catalyst of conflict and a pacifist in conflict. Wherever he went he caused people to love him or hate him. He was brutally captured, unjustly tried, beaten near death, and then stripped naked and publicly nailed to a post until he died. He had real enemies that violently and vehemently hated him. Nevertheless, he asked the Father to forgive them because they didn't know what they were doing.

Jesus' kingdom is counter-cultural to all cultures. His is an upside-down kingdom that cannot be conformed to any political agenda. Contrary to how our world operates, it is not the warmongers who will inherit the earth. Jesus said the gentle shall inherit the earth (Matt. 5:5). The kingdom of God is completely contrary to the world system. We are called to be different from the world.

For us to see a revolution in our world, we must first see a revolution of our own hearts and minds. Before we can change the world, we must first be changed ourselves.

In the first section, I unpacked the strong teachings of Galatians. We discovered how much change is needed for us to truly be free and become change agents in our world. I attempted to expose how much of our spiritual enterprise is really done by our own muscle rather than the Spirit. There are consequences to a spirituality that is based upon our own strength, and I tried to demonstrate that those are evident both in Galatians and our churches. We must choose to be filled and to walk in the Spirit and cannot gain spiritual results with fleshly methods. We saw how our passion for revolution must come from within. We also saw how we can best help our own fallen in this revolution. Finally, we addressed the true gospel spirituality available to us in Christ.

The first section was open-heart surgery to reveal how we need a revolution within. The second section revealed the heart of a revolutionary, Jesus, as he encountered the problems of this world.

If we are strong in spirit and not always reactionary to every cause, I believe we will approach the issues of our day with a more Christlike insight. I believe our priorities will be more reflective of his love and less of our own selfish agendas.

I have tried to demonstrate how Jesus would respond to some of the issues of our day. There are some issues today Jesus didn't encounter at all, so I chose not to address those with projection and theory. There is no story or message from Jesus in the gospels that addresses homosexuality, abortion, or campaign finance reform, so I did not write about those issues. I tried to show how Jesus took on some issues that are still current. I wanted to demonstrate that his ways were far different from our current reactions. While it may appear that I randomly chose these issues, I actually tried to bring out real and tangible examples from the Gospels that are relevant to how we respond to our current world. As these stories unfolded I always had in mind both Jesus' response to the issue and our own reaction, which is usually quite the opposite.

We are to bring a spiritual revolution to our culture. If we can ignite a revolution in our own lives, we will then be able to do so in our world. It is futile to attempt the latter without first addressing the former. We watched Jesus encounter those who are wealthy and those who are on welfare. We saw how he empowered women others held in contempt. We watched Jesus ignite a revolution against the consumer-driven forms of worship that empowered an elite few and held others in bondage. Finally, in this conclusion, we saw how Jesus responded (or didn't) to the mechanisms of governance.

FINALLY . . .

An interesting thing occurred while I was editing this book. Some dear friends read the book for me and offered feedback. They assumed what my view was on certain issues simply because I was not espousing their views. I was not at all saying what they thought I was. The patterns in their brain "filled in" information that I actually never wrote. I asked myself why this happened. I had one of my friends read a chapter three times and then went over it with him line by line until he saw what I was actually saying. We were not so far off in our beliefs after that. One can argue from this that I am not a good communicator, but I think there is more.

I believe we all have been programmed to hear with a bias that doesn't always allow us to actually hear what is being said. We have been force fed by media only two options and challenged to choose a side. We are so accustomed to the same sound bites on both sides that when we hear something different from our point of view our brains automatically dump the voice into the opposite category without really listening. We're programmed to defend ourselves and demonize others. We have allowed the propaganda to infiltrate our minds so much that we cannot grasp any other alternatives than the two heaped upon us constantly by media.

It is entirely possible that readers with left leaning thought this book was too conservative. It is also probable that readers that are conservative felt I was left-leaning in my thoughts. This is not bad news to me, but actually a sign of success. Why? Because you cannot put Jesus on a side. He does not fit into your categories or align with any political agenda. He will not be the Right's mascot or the Left's rallying cry. Jesus challenges all of us, wherever we are, to change. There are two sides: his or not his (Matt. 12:30). He will not be packaged to fit a typical pundit's commentary or coerced to take our side on any issue (Jos. 5:13–15).

"It was for freedom that Christ set us free" (Gal. 5:1). Free your mind and free your soul so that you, too, can be different enough to make a difference. Do not be a mouthpiece for a cause beyond Jesus. Do not let rich old white men in a room full of cigar smoke and expensive Scotch determine what you believe. A fraternity of elites in ivory towers with utopian dreams and zero tolerance of any other point of view should not determine your choice. You have Jesus as your head. Jesus is not a Republican, and he is not a Democrat. Jesus is not a capitalist or a communist. He doesn't need to vote; in fact, in the end he has the only deciding vote in his kingdom. He is the King of kings and Lord of lords. Follow him and be different so that you can change this world.

The same old thing never changed anything. There is only one thing that can truly change this world, and his name is Jesus. You can't have a one-thing spirituality and other things as well. By its very definition, a one thing is an "only thing." Pursue the one thing at the expense of everything.

Welcome to the revolution.

NOTES

Introduction

1. Lance Ford, *Revangelical: Becoming the Good News People We're Meant to Be* (Carol Stream, IL: Tyndale, 2014), 2.
2. Richard N. Longenecker, *Galatians*, Word Biblical Commentary, no. 41 (Dallas: Word Books, 1990), vii.

Chapter 1: A Tale of Two Churches

1. While we only have two of his letters in the New Testament, what is called 1 Corinthians is actually Paul's second letter to this church (1 Cor. 5:9–11), making 2 Corinthians his third letter, if not his fourth. There is a possibility that he wrote a fourth letter between what we call 1 Corinthians and 2 Corinthians. This fourth letter could be what he refers to as a severe letter, written in much sorrow (2 Cor. 2:4; 7:8). This could be a reference to 1 Corinthians, because in that letter he asserts authority in disciplining a sexually immoral man (1 Cor. 5:1–5), who appears to have repented and needed restoration in 2 Corinthians (2 Cor. 2:5–7).
2. There is no mention of the Jerusalem letter from Acts 15 in Galatians, which is hard to explain if Paul wrote the Galatian letter after the council meeting.
3. For more information about Paul's journeys and the churches he started, see Neil Cole, *Journeys to Significance: Charting a Leadership Course from the Life of Paul* (San Francisco: Jossey-Bass, 2011).
4. Alan Hirsch and Mike Frost, *The Shaping of Things to Come: Innovation and Mission for the 21st-Century Church* (Peabody, MA: Hendriksen, 2003), 28–30.

Chapter 2: Consequences of a Do-It-Yourself Spirituality

1. Mark Labberton in a message given at the Sentralized Conference, Kansas City, September 23, 2013.
2. Lance Ford, *Revangelical: Becoming the Good News People We're Meant to Be* (Carol Stream, IL: Tyndale, 2014), 31.
3. Tom Krattenmaker, *The Evangelicals You Don't Know: Introducing the Next Generation of Christians* (Lanham, MD: Rowman & Littlefield, 2013), 107.
4. Ibid.
5. Adelle M. Banks, "Poll: Nearly 80% of Americans Say They Are Christian," *Houston Chronicle,* January 5, 2012, www.chron.com/life/houston-belief/article/Poll-Nearly-80-percent-of-americans-say-they-are-244092.php.
6. Scott McKnight, *The King Jesus Gospel: The Original Good News Revisited* (Grand Rapids: Zondervan, 2011), 20.
7. Tim Keller, *Center Church: Balanced, Gospel-Centered Ministry in Your City* (Grand Rapids: Zondervan, 2012), 79.

Chapter 3: Revolutions Are Never Won on Defense

1. Stephen R. Covey, *The Seven Habits of Highly Effective People: Restoring the Character Ethic* (New York: Simon and Schuster, 1989), 65–94.
2. Neil Cole, *Organic Church: Growing Faith Where Life Happens* (San Francisco: Jossey-Bass, 2005), 10–11.
3. There is new insight emerging about the five gifts of Ephesians 4:11 and a church built on the foundation of apostles and prophets. For a sample of the new thinking on the recovery of the apostolic gift and foundation, see Neil Cole, *Primal Fire: Reigniting the Church with the Five Gifts of Jesus* (Carol Stream, IL: Tyndale, 2014); Alan Hirsch and Tim Catchim, *The Permanent Revolution: Apostolic Imagination and Practice for the 21st Century Church* (San Francisco: Jossey-Bass, 2012).
4. This description of a false apostle is from Cole, *Primal Fire*. To understand how all five gifts of Ephesians 4:11 are counterfeited, see *Primal Fire*, chapter 18.
5. R. A. Torrey, ed., *The Fundamentals: A Testimony to Truth* (Grand Rapids: Baker, 1972).

6. I devoted an entire chapter to this question in Neil Cole, *Church 3.0: Upgrades for the Future of the Church* (San Francisco: Jossey-Bass, 2000), 222–40.

7. See Neil Cole, *Ordinary Hero: Becoming a Disciple Who Makes a Difference* (Grand Rapids: Baker, 2008), 178–185, and Neil Cole, *Organic Leadership: Leading Naturally Right Where You Are* (Grand Rapids: Baker, 2009), 74–84.

Chapter 4: Lighting the Fires of Revolution

1. This motivational chart was first introduced in Neil Cole, *Search and Rescue: Becoming a Disciple Who Makes a Difference* (Grand Rapids: Baker, 2007), 86–96.

2. John Piper, *Desiring God: Meditations of a Christian Hedonist* (Portland, OR: Multnomah, 1986), 308–12.

3. Neil Cole, *Cultivating a Life for God: Multiplying Disciples Through Life Transformation Groups* (St. Charles, IL: Church Smart Resources, 1999), 30–31.

Chapter 5: Restoring Our Fallen

1. See Neil Cole, *Organic Leadership: Leading Naturally Right Where You Are* (Grand Rapids: Baker, 2009), 85–96; Neil Cole, *Primal Fire: Reigniting the Church with the Five Gifts of Jesus* (Carol Stream, IL: Tyndale, 2014), 29–54; Neil Cole and Phil Helfer, *Church Transfusion: Changing Your Church Organically—From the Inside Out* (Hoboken, NJ: Jossey-Bass, 2012), 114–28.

2. C. S. Lewis, *The Great Divorce* (San Francisco: Harper Collins, 2001), 75.

3. Benjamin Franklin, *Poor Richard's Almanack* (New York: Seedbox Press, 2011), Kindle Edition, 146.

Chapter 6: The One-Thing Spirituality

1. Tony Campolo, *Who Switched the Price Tags?* (Nashville: Thomas Nelson, 2008).

2. See Neil Cole, *Organic Church: Growing Faith Where Life Happens* (San Francisco: Jossey-Bass, 2005), 159–69.

3. Ibid., 181–84.

4. You can see a more in-depth explanation of the universal disciple pattern from Thom Wolf at www.universal-disciple.com. My good friend Curtis Sergeant is also one of the geniuses behind the uncovering of the Universal Disciple idea that Thom first revealed to me. I am indebted to both of these masterminds!

5. See Cole, *Organic Church,* chapter 8 for a more detailed discussion of the New Testament discipleship pattern, 109–21.

6. I have written a couple of books that present a tool for making disciples that encompasses all of the universal disciple pattern in a highly reproducible manner. The method is called Life Transformation Groups. See Neil Cole, *Cultivating a Life for God: Multiplying Disciples through Life Transformation Groups* (St. Charles, IL: Church Smart Resources, 1999) and Neil Cole, *Search and Rescue: Becoming a Disciple Who Makes a Difference* (Grand Rapids, MI: Baker, 2007) (also titled *Ordinary Hero*).

Chapter 7: Jesus Takes on Wealth

1. Emma Seery et al., "Even It Up: Time to End Extreme Inequality," http://www.oxfamamerica.org/static/media/files/even-it-up-inequality-oxfam.pdf, p. 6.

2. A lecture by Dallas Willard presented at the Anaheim Vineyard, Anaheim, California, 2000.

3. From a radio interview answering the question "Is it okay for Christians to be rich?" November 5, 2014.

4. I find that Luke's gospel builds this story best, but for our purposes, we will draw from the other gospels as well.

Chapter 8: Jesus Takes on Welfare

1. George R. Beasley-Murray, *John*, Word Biblical Commentary, vol. 36, 2nd ed. (Nashville: Thomas Nelson, 1999), 155.

2. William Barclay, *The Gospel of John*, vol. 2, The Daily Bible Study (Philadelphia: Westminster Press, 1975), 44–45.

Chapter 9: Jesus Takes on Women in Crisis

1. William Barclay, *The Gospel of John*, vol. 1, New Daily Study Bible, (Louisville: Westminster John Knox, 1975), Kindle Edition, 189.

2. Ibid., 195.
3. https://twitter.com/branthansen/status/533334421936435201. Used by permission.
4. https://www.facebook.com/rachelheldevans.page/posts/10152630836214442. Used by permission.

Chapter 10: Jesus Takes on Worship

1. Alan Hirsch in a message delivered in Dallas, TX, September 2014. Used by permission.
2. http://www.examiner.com/article/joel-osteen-s-followers-give-32-million-a-year-church-theft-reveals-offerings.
3. Alan Hirsch and Debra Hirsch, *Untamed: Reactivating a Missional Form of Discipleship* (Grand Rapids, MI: Baker, 2010), 47.

ABOUT THE AUTHOR

Neil Cole is an experienced church planter and pastor. In addition to founding the Organic Church Movement, he is a founder of Church Multiplication Associates (CMA), which over the past fifteen years has grown to tens of thousands of churches in all fifty states and in fifty-plus nations.

An international speaker, Neil has also authored twelve books.

Currently, Neil serves as CMA's executive director and is responsible for resourcing church leaders with ministry tools to reproduce healthy disciples, leaders, churches, and movements. His responsibilities also include developing, training, assessing, and coaching church planters.

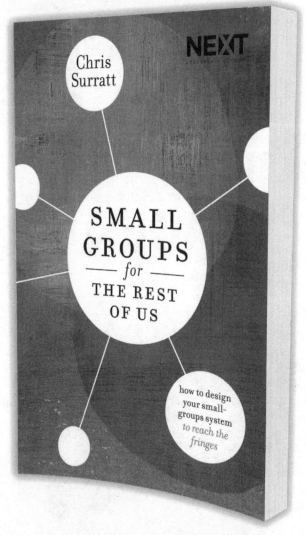